ALSO BY TONI MORRISON

Fiction

The Bluest Eye
Sula
Song of Solomon
Tar Baby
Beloved
Jazz
Paradise
Love
A Mercy
Home
God Help the Child
Recitatif

Nonfiction

Playing in the Dark
The Origin of Others
The Source of Self-Regard

Language as Liberation

Language as Liberation

Reflections on the American Canon

TONI MORRISON

Introduction and Notes
by Claudia Brodsky

ALFRED A. KNOPF   New York

2026

A BORZOI BOOK
FIRST HARDCOVER EDITION PUBLISHED
BY ALFRED A. KNOPF 2026

Published by Alfred A. Knopf, a division of Penguin Random House LLC, 1745 Broadway, New York, NY 10019.

Knopf, Borzoi Books, and the colophon are registered trademarks of Penguin Random House, LLC.

Syllabus: Toni Morrison Papers, C1491, Manuscripts Division, Department of Special Collections, Princeton University Library

Library of Congress Cataloging-in-Publication Data
Names: Morrison, Toni, 1931–2019 author |
Brodsky, Claudia, [date] writer of introduction
Title: Language as liberation : reflections on the American canon /
Toni Morrison; introduction and notes by Claudia Brodsky.
Description: First edition. | New York: Alfred A. Knopf, 2026. |
Includes index.
Identifiers: LCCN 2025016670 (print) | LCCN 2025016671 (ebook) |
ISBN 9780593802748 (hardcover) | ISBN 9780593802755 (ebook)
Subjects: LCSH: American literature—History and criticism |
Canon (Literature) | LCGFT: Literary criticism | Lectures
Classification: LCC PS124 .M65 2026 (print) | LCC PS124 (ebook) |
DDC 810.9—dc23/eng/20250418
LC record available at https://lccn.loc.gov/2025016670
LC ebook record available at https://lccn.loc.gov/2025016671

penguinrandomhouse.com | aaknopf.com

Printed in the United States of America
1st Printing

The authorized representative in the EU for product safety and compliance is Penguin Random House Ireland, Morrison Chambers, 32 Nassau Street, Dublin D02 YH68, Ireland, https://eu-contact.penguin.ie.

For Safa and Nidal
You are the light in every chapter of my life.

—F.M.

Contents

On Toni Morrison's Teaching and Lectures

This book grew from the belief that my mother's teaching materials, her lectures, essays, and notes to students, deserve to stand with her published work. They were written for the classroom, where she believed the glorious world of thinking and teaching happened in real time, and where language could still surprise.

She asked her students to meet the writing where it lived, without shortcuts, without softening. That same intensity threads through every page here.

The bracketed notes we've kept in italics are like hearing her think to herself, catching the spark of a thought as she shaped a class or a line of argument.

I want to thank Claudia Brodsky, who taught alongside my mother and brought her real insight, her congruent ideology and care to this project. Her notes, essays, and framing help give the audience a sense of how these writings came to be and how they still matter.

—FORD MORRISON

Course Description for "Studies in American Africanism" —Toni Morrison

An examination of ways in which the American literary tradition has responded to an Africanistic presence in the United States. Concentrating on authors who have imagined, explored, represented, and employed the narrative, the personae, and the idiom of Africans and their descendants, the course will analyze the fictional strategies designed to accommodate Africanism; the imaginative uses to which African-Americans are put; the manner in which these engagements clarify the idea of an American "self."

The Literary departures of certain American writers into what was perceived to be a separate culture constitute subtle and highly creative engagements with and within the literature. The manner in which such departures inform the text and require alternative fictional strategies to accommodate an African-American presence is instructive.

The course will examine selected works to locate these strategies,* the imaginative uses to which African-Americans were put, and ways in

---

* The typescripts of these lectures included page citations to texts Toni Morrison was teaching from. It is unknown which editions of course books she was referring to at all times, but we have kept these page numbers to preserve her work on the page as it was written. — F.M.

which these literary forays into Africanism contribute to the evolution of the American "self" in the literature. Discussions will analyze (a) textual formulations of Africanism, (b) Africanism as informing incumbent of the text, and (c) how the intertextual presences of African-Americans illuminate the American "self."

—T.M.

Introduction

History and Literature:
The Metaphysics of Race in America

Claudia Brodsky

To read Morrison's *Reflections on the American Canon* is to reconceive the establishment of the canon of American fiction, no less than of the nation itself, as founded on the basis of something called "race."

When it comes to the history of the nation, those racial rules of establishment are plainly stated. An early example of "democratic" realpolitik, the constitutionally enshrined "three-fifths" rule stipulated a statistical division within the definition of enslaved persons. Designed to appease slaveholders and abolitionists alike, that Solomonic splitting of the proverbial baby worked. On one hand, enslaved persons would henceforth count as persons, while, on the other, as property, according to a prescribed ratio of legal to fiscal standing to which all participating parties agreed. Acknowledged as a "peculiar compromise" by its inventor, James Madison, that proportional division provided the fledgling federal government with the tax revenue it needed to exist, and the slave-holding states with the congressional power they needed to persist. It achieved this double objective by way of an indeed peculiar, not to say impossible, purely quantitative fiction. Stranger than the notion of the man-*like* machine imagined some decades earlier by the father of all cyborg fantasies, the Enlightenment materialist theorist, Julien Offray de La Mettrie, internal and foundational to the literally eponymous Constitution of the United States was the wholly artificial constitution of a "numerically" fractured being, a legal fabrication designed to be "considered by our laws, in some respects, as persons, in other respects, as property." The *subject* of this doubly constitutional fiction was no eighteenth-century dream of the fully automated imitation of life that has returned to enchant for-profit markets today, but the wholly human Africans every aspect of whose lives colonial markets found it opportune to enslave, previously for the mutual benefit both of their own capitalization and that of their British "trading partners," now for their own "independent" expansion and wildly extravagant profit.

The agreement of otherwise opposed signatories to the American Constitution was thus predicated upon the creation of a kind of science fiction or hybrid being, part human, part machine. "Viewed" in "the Federal Constitution . . . in the mixt character of persons and of property," Africans and their descendants were thus explicitly defined by its foundational text to perform a dual function within the life of the nation. What is routinely forgotten and most important to recall in the apparently interminable, intentionally distracting "debate" over whether race-based discrimination "defines"—rather than remains the single most potent political tool employed across—the United States, or, if it does, whether all ethnic populations who have ever constituted the nation are not equally subject to its consequences, is that the personhood of *Africans alone* is not only explicitly written into the nation to equal less than that of all other peoples to begin with, but that the *use value* of doing so is just as explicitly spelled out in the Constitution itself. In other words, the "peculiar compromise" assigning enslaved Africans and their descendants the impossibly "mixt character" enabling their computation as "person" or "property" according to an optimized ratio reflected no theoretical or "philosophical" premise, but, rather, a purely pragmatic—economic *and* political—calculation usurping any such epistemological or moral consideration. Legally redefining enslaved people as "three-fifths" or 60 percent of a *person* (while effectively denying them 100 percent of the rights the same Constitution accorded to persons) for the sole purpose of including them within the national census count, this arithmetic solution to the problem of achieving national unification, realized on the bent backs of the enslaved, ensured slaveowners a disproportionately large number of representatives in Congress (in relation to states without enslaved populations). Conversely, by legally redefining the remaining two-fifths or 40 percent of enslaved people as *property,* it ensured the inclusion of their cumulative market value within the estimation of the property tax owed the nation by slaveowners. Rendered acceptable by its apparently neutral mathematical expression, this monstrous amphibology, or self-contradictory categorization of a racially defined set of human beings as at once people *and* property, was merely the ultimate reductio ad absurdum of the very proposition on which the institution of slavery—of forcibly transporting, selling, buying, and owning people *as if* they were things, machines exclusively purposed to produce and reproduce labor for others' benefit—rested.

Thus it is that, with the exception of the imaginary geographies perennially occupying the brains of all phenotypical varietals of "white" supremacism everywhere, alongside those actual states of the United States anachronistically "banning" its reality, there are few precincts in the world where the fact that American history has been cast, directed, and enacted on a stage constructed of prescribed intraspecies hierarchies is *not* common knowledge. Nor are the real-life scenarios in which some persons must quite literally suffer—their bodies *and* minds compelled to bear the burden of ensuring—the prosperity and well-being of others, or the fact that, unlike any other nation, the "united" states alone declared war on and slaughtered each other (at the highest known rate in history) over the "question" (i.e., sanctified "natural law" of domination to some, obscene abomination of both men and nature to others) of whether the then already two-centuries-old establishment of domestic slavery should not only continue but *expand* from southern into western states.

This history may indeed be so well known as to be ignored, overlooked, or immediately pushed aside by the short-sighted orientation of our minds toward present sense perception. But *literature,* which is to say, fictions declaring themselves to be such, are by definition and in principle a very distinct matter from either historical fact or transitory empirical perception and require the very different mode of mental orientation involved in the act of *reading* (words), rather than *perceiving* (phenomena), in order to be understood, let alone conceived as known by any reader at all. Morrison, a newly canonized master of American and, moreover and most significantly, world literature, reads the canon she has joined as at once upholding *and* radically undercutting that clear distinction. The basis for this apparent paradox is laid bare by the lectures themselves. For over and above the fact that all history and literature share a common medium—the language required to compose, record, and transmit them—the dividing line separating fact from fiction in their American formation is crossed at the specific pseudo-empirical crux uniting them. From the start, that crucial point of intersection between history and fiction binds together as it also divides "the American story." While shaped by its own narrative style and content, every fiction representing that story reflects the fiction at its foundation: the immeasurably "peculiar," *because* arithmetically measured, "compromise" that made it possible for the first self-authored nation to write itself into existence. At once flatly unnatural and dehumanizing on its face, the "three-fifths" formula proffered to all present the great artificial advantage of simultaneously confusing and maintaining the essential epistemological division between persons and things. In so doing it created the fractured contractual basis for opposing proto-states to unite just long enough to ratify the constitutional establishment of the United States.

This nationally unifying *division* of the lives and bodies of enslaved people into part person, part property was both a conceptual coup and no mere convenient fiction. A self-evident paradox embraced for the sake of a single goal, it also literally divided the referential map of the nation. The consequences of that mortally real geographical division would again be borne solely by those human beings artificially subjected to their own expeditious redefinition. In the blunt terms legalized by this paradox in the flesh, any person understood as African by birth or descent would henceforth be considered either a "who" or a "what" depending on which side of artificially drawn boundary lines that person was situated within. As if to reiterate the bizarre nature of the reality so created, the "border states"—literally so-called to designate a delimited state of impermanent indeterminacy *between* sides—effectively marked with a symbolic "x" the constant variable of a makeshift equation whose true value (free or unfree, person or property) remained ever to be determined at some later date.

The brutal historical facts and enduring factual conditions embodying and ensuing from that originally divided contractual definition include the ongoing de facto segregation of virtually every corner of American geography, and with it, we readily forget, each potential American author's imagination. Whether by (illegal) neighborhood "covenant" or informal sidestepping of anti-discrimination laws, the nation's now virtual border states continue to shift and, in many cases, shrink, with all the violent consequences of inequitable property values that such divisions within an increasingly capital-centric society entail, including but not limited to government and private investment, public and private services, and, across all of these, policing. Greater property values lead to greater funding—for education, housing, medical facilities, civic, cultural, and commercial spaces—just as decreasing tax values engulf all of the above in a death spiral. Living in the much-vaunted here and now, we see and know this to be the case, disapprove of or openly laud and enforce it, usually without considering (or caring) how "here" became here, and "now" became now. As admittedly difficult as it is to live both in the present tense and in history, there is another now, another here made available to us in the present experience of reading literature.

This is Morrison's, and every serious writer's, understanding of their verbal craft. But in Morrison's case, that understanding comes with a very particular history. Interminably rehearsing its founding "compromise," even as it repeatedly oscillates between taking either side of it, the undeletable nature of this conflicted history makes itself evident not only in the content but in the external evaluations of American literature. As literacy was denied to slaves, so from its inception was the formation of the American canon denied to their descendants, even as the actual content of American literature remained as internally divided and reflective of that division as American history. In the original words of Frederick Douglass, the most eloquent autodidact, autobiographer, and advocate of literacy in American history, born into and arduously escaped from slavery, one name for that constitutive dividing line is "the color line." Its other colloquial name is, of course, race. But what exactly, Morrison asks us to consider in these lectures—in a radically different, because truly questioning way—*is* "race"? "*Is*" it, indeed, at all, in the same empirically objective manner underwriting our knowledge of both persons and things? And if it does not exist in any real, categorical way commensurate with the dividing "line" it has come to represent, what, and, moreover, *why*, do we conceive it to do so?

Now, fiction may appear to many the last human endeavor in which to seek answers to so consequential a question. Literature—critics, from conventional Aristotelians through the most rigorous theorists of the ideological underpinnings of culture, agree—is the most ineluctable of all products of imagination. In part, this is because its medium, language, is, of all means of representation, the most abstract, and thus, also, the most subjectively "malleable." Yet at the same time, every language is, by definition, intersubjective in its very structure: no language belongs to any one user of it alone. This makes it, of all forms of expression, the most resistant to internal ideological determination, let alone externally imposed control. Morrison's thesis regarding not only what could be euphemistically called the meaningful presence of race, but the *meaning* of that very presence in American literature, does not diverge from that view, as ancient and new as the history and existence of literature itself. The precision and wealth of imaginative experimentation in language that empower and enrich her own fictions, expanding each reader's comprehension in reading them, contradict any presupposition or assertion otherwise. Morrison, in short, does *not* argue, in these probing lectures, that race—in the form of racist or racialist ideology—usurps or limits the practically undelimitable power of the imagination in the crafting of fiction. The originality of Morrison's thinking, with respect to the composition of specifically American fiction, lies, by contrast, in its theoretical *and* practical contention that imagination and race do not contradict but rather supplement each other within the constitution of a constitutively divided nation's literature. Indeed, like the pragmatic calculation of the incalculable use value of Africans in the creation of American history, the imagined presence of Africans, Morrison argues, has been of equally indelible utility in the creation of American fiction.

At the core of that argument remains the deeper, more dangerous question of what or, indeed, *whether* what we call "race" is. Morrison's irreducible answer is that it is itself a fiction: a "discourse" that continues to inscribe itself in both American history and literature. Indeed, the two discursive fields may be no more closely intertwined than in their common use and abuse of concepts of "race." It is this she has in mind when she states in lecture five, with regard to Flannery O'Connor's remarkable story "The Artificial Nigger":

> Had I not had to submit a course title respectable enough to pass
> muster with the Committee on Academic Instruction, I would

have called this course, or subtitled it, the same title Flannery O'Connor gave to the story by her I've asked you to read.

Apparently Miss O'Connor believed it her most satisfactory story. It isn't mine . . . but for the purposes of this discussion, it is as perfect and as perfectly written as a short piece of fiction can be—both identifying the thesis of this course and dramatizing that thesis. (Morrison, p. 67)

The "thesis" Morrison has in mind is perfectly encapsulated in O'Connor's title because, beginning with the definite article ("The"), its three juxtaposed words indeed perfectly express the (fictive) reality of race in America. A merely superficial (*if* that), thoroughly nonscientific mode of primarily social categorization, contradicted at every turn by the singular chromosomal composition of the entire human species, that reality requires the invention and circulation of an additional pejorative label created to designate, and so single out and isolate as other-than-human, those humans of whom societies—or the private and state-sponsored companies promoted by their respective societies—had already presumed to dispose at will. What is extraordinary about this particular pejorative label or epithet, as Hemingway's pointed use of it in *To Have and Have Not*—the subject of Morrison's fourth lecture—makes especially clear, is the self-reinforcing work it does for and in the minds of its users. All forms of insult, the founder of speech act theory observed, are just as much acts of language as are standard performative statements: words which *do* something (that they alone can do), like "I promise," "I bet," "I bequeath," "I do," rather than report or refer to something or state of affairs that exists independently of language itself. However, what distinguishes the work performed by the n-word and other group epithets, including all collective gender, religion, and ethnicity insults, is the *double* work they do. For while personal insults, directed at a particular individual, point outward, depersonalizing group epithets point in two directions at once. At the same time as they target individuals, they effectively reverse that external vector of reference by turning the outside inside, referring any empirical person so named—near or far, young or old, indeed, living or dead—*back* to the group insult to which he or she is instead subordinated. Rather than using words to name, describe, and give meaning to individual people, group pejoratives use individual people to feed their entirely imaginary generic meaning, without which reversal of meaning, from person to word, the group epithet would necessarily mean nothing at all. In short: in the collective version of the personal epithet, the person belongs to the insult, rather than the insult to the person.

Such is the mental action of derogatory generalizations repeated and amplified in each instance of their empirical application. The act of dehumanization performed in the act of pejorative designation (what Austin called an "illocutionary act," or speech that does something "*in*" the act of saying something), thus constitutes a kind of semantic loop, in which the referent (here, an actual person) toward which a word is directed serves instead to represent *it.* A mentally fabricated label requiring empirical referents to sustain it: such are the linguistic mechanics without which racism could not exist. For racism cannot be reduced to any one physical action. It is instead the general mental framework that enables every such action, and language is the mode by which that mental framework *communicates itself*—as indeed it must. For its quality as a general conception, functioning in advance and full independence of each empirical context, is to encompass any and every imaginable instance of its application.

Thus it is that O'Connor's title not only serves up the flatly "artificial" existence of the racist epithet but, both most stunningly and accurately, declares that existence in the singular. For every use of the n-word similarly defines ("the") one to stand for all. And since no such emblematic nonhuman human can or could ever exist in reality, every designation of such a notional being is at the same time a pure act of symbolization: each and any subject referenced by and referred back to the n-word is "artificial," *someone made into something made in the mind of its designator.* Yet the power of the collective epithet also exceeds that of its speaker. As the conclusion of O'Connor's story lays bare, every private production of a general symbol serves a still more powerful social function. When a backwoods white grandfather's plan to stage his grandson's first, presumably terrifying encounter with black people on a visit to multiracial Atlanta backfires, further straining the intergenerational bond forged in racism it was intended to strengthen, it is the final sudden sight of a decrepit lawn jockey that provides the grandfather the pretext he needs to fill that generational gap. And what he fills it with is the n-word, grasped at like a life raft in a shipwreck of his own making. And, at least at this concluding moment, the life raft floats: the group epithet not only extricates its exclaimer from the dangerous attractions of the *diverse* reality that now surrounds him, but provides this otherwise illiterate grandfather with the single shared, *verbal* ground on which to reunite with his grandson.

Thus the promise of generational change, of the difference of history itself, collapses under the force of a tried-and-true speech act. Yet, at the same time as the group epithet serves to unite its users across time and place, it effectively reduces them to mere conduits for the symbolic action already provided and confirmed by the social lexicon. In sum, and as any speaker, writer, hearer, or reader of it instinctively knows, every use of the n-word (or any other collective epithet) not only is, but, moreover, *is meant to be* a speech act. Furthermore, unlike other conventional speech acts, whose words ("I promise," "I do") announce the act they first bring about, the racist epithet acts to make artifice masquerade as a neutral statement of fact. Still, to say that not only the racial epithets that name it, but that "race" as such is, in Morrison's words, a "discourse"—not a definitive thing but a linguistic fiction—is to raise the further question of what kind of fiction, what kind of language, it is. What form of artificial discursive "construct" has the power to appeal to the imagination in such a way as to shape not only an entire nation's empirical history but the individual imaginations of the most formidable authors of its literature?

In that fiction runs so deep, and includes so many layers, it can be difficult to determine where any meaningful attempt to unravel them should begin. Operating on a supposedly "innate" or biological level is the fiction that race is a clearly perceptible empirical characteristic—something we "know" when we "see" it. The historical inadequacy, not to say the studied stupidity, of such a "view" is belied by the self-evident paradox at the heart of the weirdly always ready-to-hand "one-drop rule" invoked by executors of genocide and racial segregation alike. That purity test of last resort at once forces *and* begs the question that the very concept of race raises from the start. For, if, unlike culture or ethnicity, race is an empirical fact knowable on its face, why would its recognition require an epidemiological fiction? For, modeling itself on the study of disease, the "one-drop rule" purports to distinguish the single contaminating molecule within a vital fluid that is, by definition, everywhere self-identical: that "one" among a living body's uncountable, because incessantly self-replenishing, store of blood cells, somehow demonstrative of a single sliver of its inherently heterogeneous history. If race is simultaneously understood as something both immediately perceptible and elusive of detection—both superficial and requiring investigation beyond all "skin-deep" perceptions—then it can be no thing, nor even any discernible quality or condition, but rather, as Morrison concludes, can only be "an *idea*," which, like any idea, can only be made present *to the mind* by its representation in discourse. In her lecture on *Absalom, Absalom!*, Faulkner's most unstinting, capaciously written, step-by-step demonstration, in interconnecting intensely detailed, individually constructed narrative fictions, of the "national tragedy" enacted daily by that "discourse," Morrison states:

> If race cannot be *seen*, Faulkner shows us, then it must be something else, something other than its markers. This "other-than-its-

markers" is what the novel requires us to search for, to contemplate. If race is hidden, and we are forced to *find* it, then we learn not much about race, but a great deal about racist discourse. Faulkner serves up to us this racist discourse in all its futility, madness, incoherence, and obsessiveness. Thus it is not race, but the discourse of race that menaces, ruins, paralyzes, corrupts, and annihilates. And paradoxically, it is the *discourse* that both represses and searches out race. Formulated in speech, memories, recapitulations, letters, dialogue, and monologues, the discourse of race, its narrative practices, the *idea* of race, and the construction of whiteness are exposed as sources of national tragedy. (Morrison, p. 150)

Now, any *"idea"* irreducible to visible "markers," indeed to physical manifestations of any kind, which compels us to "search [it] out," is properly called "metaphysical." What these lectures and the fictions Morrison explores in them suggest is that the creation of America—a nation that, beginning with its own origin *in discourse,* defined itself not only to possess the most transcendental of all ideas, freedom, but the unprecedented freedom to make itself—entailed a very particular twist on metaphysics: a *nationally* transcendental counter-notion of unfreedom that its own realization of freedom required in order to become an object of experience on earth. That is to say, for freedom to be made the basis not of any individual's capacity for what Kant was first to call "self-legislating," and thus "moral," instead of externally calculating action, but of the self-legitimizing establishment and pursuant actions of an entire nation of persons of unequal legal entitlement and means, unfreedom would have to be established as a metaphysical principle alongside it. And while the *idea* of freedom, by definition—as Jean-Jacques Rousseau would be the first to recognize—negates the ability of any historical action or condition to negate *it,* the freedom of a *nation* written into existence under the auspices of the same must define itself by negating not only what but *who* is not its subject. As Morrison argues across these lectures, the "idea of race" thus accompanies the idea of freedom in American literature not as its absence or negation, but, on the contrary, as its positively enabling negative condition.

In sum, the definitively metaphysical, because essentially undelimitable, idea of freedom, when posited as the "universal" principle of a new, already internally divided nation, may have indeed required an overlay of arithmetic artifice to disguise the absolute, artificially irresoluble contradiction, of human beings free to make other human beings unfree, that this nation embodied. But what is written as a metaphysically *and* materially impossible ratio into the contractual birth of the nation is also fated to become a mode of literary representation in the life of the nation. And in this the "American story" distinguishes itself both from other nations' fictions and from their histories. For the conquest and extermination or resettlement of the population already inhabiting the land that the fledgling nation of transatlantic invaders would claim as its own to exploit repeated as if by rote the murderous model of territorial appropriation that has undergirded every civilization before it similarly bent on expanding its dominion. But what made the celebrated American "experiment" unique was its founding canonization of both immortal freedom and existential unfreedom, the "inalienable rights" of the men who proclaimed those rights *and* the transatlantic importation in chains of men and women denied every conceivable right.

Just as the ways in which that foundational contradiction in terms continues to define the nation grounded in it, so in the literature born with that contradiction, its representation takes every imaginable form. One of these is the notion of America itself as perpetually existing under the shadow it just as perpetually projects ahead of and behind itself. That shadow emerges differently in the discourse of every work analyzed by Morrison in these lectures. Sometimes it is clearly and directly represented (as in the fictions of Stowe and McCullers, or, to opposite yet, among them, very different effect, in those of Hemingway and Stein); sometimes it takes stark, while indirect, form (as in the radically constrictive, and thus effectively self-incriminating, narrative perspective of the single, self-centered slaveholder adopted by Cather); sometimes it is artfully represented as the fiction driving the stories that the authors themselves are compelled to tell (as in the extremely stylistically divergent, yet equally critically self-conscious cases of Twain, O'Connor, and Faulkner); and, finally, sometimes it takes apparently unconscious but no less compulsive forms (as in the cases of Poe, Bellow, and Styron).

One allegorical figure for this shadow, cited by Morrison, is of America itself as a "Dark House": the bearer and source of the long shadow of race, the uncannily unifying division between fantasy and reality it both projects and protects. As Morrison reveals, this was the title Faulkner had originally assigned, first, to the various fictions that would become *Light in August* (pub. 1932), and, next, to the most aesthetically and critically formidable of all his creations, *Absalom, Absalom!* (pub. 1936). Interpreting that "darkness" as a metaphysical condition related by the openly anti-segregationist and anti-fascist Faulkner to the foundational American taboo called "race," Morrison exposes the literary function of the controlling "fear" of this supposed darkness, and resulting construction-in-progress of America's own terrified and terrifying "Dark House." As she observes of the various incarnations of the "idea" of such a house across Faulkner's fictions:

> All of these images . . . illuminate some idea in Faulkner's imagination about a house or entity that is dark as in secret or dark as in sullied or dark as in menaced by what is the single most obvious factor in all of these stories: race, specifically the black race. The Africanist persona writ large. (Morrison, p. 147)

Probing further into the image of the "dark house," as site of an already divided defense against race, built to be most impregnable when race itself is undetectable, Morrison offers an analysis of the story of Thomas Sutpen's own metaphysical conception of race in

Absalom, Absalom!—and with it, American history's—as *most present when absent* (and for that purely ideational reason, relentlessly "threatening"), that can be seen to stand in many ways for the extraordinary insight informing these lectures as a whole:

> So if in Faulkner's imagination the patriarch's house is *dark,* it is a signal for alarm. The modifier alerts us to this absence of light as an alteration, a disfigurement—something gone awry, turning the house away from its purpose—the maintenance of control against disorder and chance; turning it instead to that which is sinister, disorderly, destined, and corrupt. It is a darkness that disturbs genealogy, disrupts its planned progression by distorting, deferring, and repeating it in unacceptable ways. The house designed for unity is disunified by the same darkness that hides its internal divisions. The darkness of the house threatens to jump the barriers between the public and the private, and render helpless the walls of the fortress against the values imposed by the public. Thus the goal of privacy becomes the urgent need for secrecy. Darkness then is both fear of disorder and a necessary strategy; a rejection and a requirement. (Morrison, p. 149)

As Faulkner's devastatingly clear-eyed imagination moves us to recognize, so Morrison's undaunted analyses demonstrate that the "darkness of the house"—the shadow, present absence or negation, that the nation carries within and around it, as a metaphysically illimitable and physically delimiting "idea of race," as of freedom from the same—lives on in the language of its canonical literature, no less than the discourse of its governing laws. And while the physical side of that negation begins, it does not end with the right to live free of corporal violation. For having already been alienated by unrelenting violence applied to their bodies from the freedom defining the being of every human being from birth, those enslaved for profit and pleasure unto death face the additional condition of absolute unfreedom beyond death, in the ongoing lives of their offspring. And as that imaginary darkness, that negation of freedom imposed from within upon an integral other imagined instead as outside it—the effort, as impotent as it is relentless, to delimit and therein take imaginary positive possession of freedom itself—continues to persist in the spirit of the nation, so does the rule of race itself denied as it is ever more expressly enforced, affirmed as it is ever more roundly decried, along ever-retraceable dividing, be they state districting or international border, local precinct, employment, or supermarket lines.

Morrison's own most famous fiction, *Beloved,* faces that real historical fact of immortal unfreedom foursquare. Unprecedented in its own loving re-creation, in language as magnificent as it is terrifying, of American lives lived in the daily struggle to survive their own negation, before and after death, *Beloved* both constituted a new apogee of world fiction and transformed the national perspective on American fiction, providing an unparalleled vantage point from which to view the traditional canon, what it does and does not represent. Of the fictions of America which it succeeded, many are represented and re-interpreted by Morrison here. Whether intentionally or reflexively employing it to shape the actions they narrate, to set those actions into relief, or merely to fill their background with faceless bodies, these classic works of the American literary canon, much like their singular legal counterpart, the Constitution, are not only informed by race, but reveal, over and over again, its imagination-ready metaphysical dimension, the unlimited historical *and* literary uses to which the concept of race can be put precisely because it names no empirically determinate reality. The *idea* of race that American fictions reify or reveal, demystify or further mythologize, is the all-too-real subject of Morrison's critically penetrating, always linguistically sensitive, intensely imagined lectures here. They ask their reader to pay equally close attention to the words of which the national imagination is made, thereby ensuring that, together with the writing of American history, the history of American literature continues to live and be read today.

Language as Liberation

Image of Blacks in Western Art

S tudies in American Africanism is an investigation into two principal areas of discursive practice: one area involves the ways in which a non-white, Africanist presence and persona was constructed in the United States; the second area involves the ways in which that fabricated "presence" served the literary imagination in its exploration of American identity.

The course uses the terms "Africanism" and "Africanist" to suggest the mythic construct of a denotative and connotative blackness, and an entire range of views, assumptions, readings, and mis-readings of African peoples and their descendants in this country. Africanism is also the process of alienizing and exoticizing one's own experience of Black people in order to know and therefore own that experience. [*caveat*] The course is not limited to an investigation of what might be called racist or non-racist literature. Nor does the course take or encourage a position that confines itself to measuring the quality of a work based on the attitudes of the author, or the representations he or she makes of another racial or ethnic group. Such judgments can and are being made in recent literary criticisms. (For example, the critical scholarship of Ezra Pound, [Louis-Ferdinand] Céline, George Jean Nathan, Paul de Man, etc.; and we know books are constantly being banned from library shelves for these alleged attitudes or representations or sensibilities regardless of past evaluations of the quality of the text. In fact, the argument has been advanced that, in the case of Paul de Man, say, or Mark Twain, the work can have no unmitigated quality precisely because the work—or in some cases not the work but the author—has been found to reveal insensitivity to ethnic, religious, sexual, or racial groups.)

However, although those judgments are within the reach of this course, they are not within its purview. One of the reasons the course does not close with analyses leading toward conclusions about a work's being racist or non-racist is that such an analysis can be an intellectual cul-de-sac—once the evidence is in, there is nothing more to be said about the work.

What we propose to do is a series of close readings of traditional American fiction in order to discover what impact notions of racial hierarchy, racial exclusion, and racial vulnerability and availability have had on the literature. We will describe and analyze how this literature has behaved in its encounter with racial ideology and discover in what ways the literature has been shaped by that encounter.

Now in order to do this we will have to identify the instances during which American literature has been complicit in the development of racialism, and when it has intervened in racial discourse to undermine or explode it; but we will want to move beyond stark identification to the further investigation of what Africanism has meant for the work/product of the writer's imagination. How does literary utterance arrange itself when it tries to imagine an Africanistic "other"? What does the encounter with Africans and/or African-Americans do to and for the work? How does one describe the rhetorical struggle that follows? Our study averts the gaze from the racialized object to the racialized subject; from the described and imagined to the describers and imaginers.

If Africanism is a construct, if "blackness" has "meaning," then so does "whiteness." One goal, then, becomes to discover how the concept of "whiteness" was built/invented/produced and what it is for. The insights we come up with may help us to discover not only the nature—even the cause of "whiteness"—but also the part that its development played in the evolution of something known, loosely, as an American. Reading and critiquing American literature from this point of view may also release the literature from the incoherence that the studied indifference and historical evasion in criticism has imposed on it. In other words, we will regard the literary engagements with Africanism as self-reflexive—as ways to talk about, imagine, and set forth/assert the deep concerns white writers have about themselves and the world they inhabit. Further, we will regard the presence of Africanism in a work as an impinging force in the execution of that work's structure and figurative language.

The suspicion of the course is that the intrusion or inclusion of Africanistic characters is significant. That the writer's choice to include or the necessity of inclusion can be shown sometimes to throttle the text, destabilize it, and, far more frequently than one would think, it can be shown to liberate it, to provide and force astonishing kinds of artistic creativity, astonishing leaps into otherwise forbidden territory, and that in the wake of this imaginative encounter, some interesting patterns emerge—patterns that should be included in the history of American literature as part of its distinguishing features.

Two points require underscoring (one about knowledge and imagination, the other about language):

1) Although we will see that "knowing" the "other"— the conviction that one "knows" Africans and African-Americans—is central to the construction of "whiteness" (knowing is, after all, the demonstration of power), we should not ever assume that the Africans and African-Americans encountered in this fiction are in fact known—they are imagined. Sartre's description of colonialist language captures the point: "These phrases (terminology

for the suborned natives) were never the translation of a real, concrete thought; they were not even the object of thought . . . they have not by themselves any meaning, at least in so far as they claim to express knowledge about the colonialized." So we will not be looking for "real" or realistic representations of blacks within a construct based on stereotypes. ("Representation is how we make our will known.") In the absence of race-neutral knowledge, or open-minded inquiry about Africans and African-Americans, and in the presence of ideological and imperialistic rationales for oppression, an invented, fictive Africanist persona emerged, and flourished because of its serviceability. Political serviceability, of course, and economic serviceability, etc.; but it is the literary serviceability that we will focus on.

The Matter of Africanism, by which I mean the fabrication of an Africanistic Presence that would support, promulgate, and enhance the institution of slavery and the hierarchy of race, seems to be a dominant figuration within American literature. And it is impor-tant to remember that under the constraints of this fabrication, we can be only secondarily concerned here with the way Africans really were—what their various cultures, laws, languages, and art forms were; nor with what African-Americans were or are really like—what kind of cultural, linguistic, artistic, and social forms they either pre-served or created in the New World. "Real" Blacks "out of the loop." In short, we are not concerned here, except indirectly, with all of what was available for these writers to see and interpret, but rather with what they believed they saw, or wished to see, and how in fact they did interpret a black "other" in their midst.

We will try to discover how the variables of racism—biologic, eco-nomic, ideological, metaphoric, metaphysical—can be understood in each of these formulations to be insistently self-referential for both the racist and the non-racist alike.

Because our route takes us repeatedly to and through economical, ideological, iconographical, and figurative racism, the order of the readings is not based on a work's date of publication or progressive literary periods. I don't want linear or chronological time to suggest a conventional "progress" in these matters. Or lead us to believe that because the language and iconography of Africanism has altered, that its force is weakened in the literature.

Roughly put, we will treat the content of sample literature like the results of a Rorschach test, the meditation on a black spot that appears in any of an unlimited variety of shapes, and hazard some speculations about what that meditation reveals about the viewer, and how he or she translates these meditations into art. Writers produce meaning in their work—and we want to note how. In some instances the act of imagining blacks produces language and images reinforced by received, unquestioned, culturally informed perceptions—perceptions, biases, and evaluations already established as "knowledge" and distributed as such. In other instances the presence of Africans and/or African-Americans alters the work—forces it away from its announced and/or hidden course and yields fresh insights that are at odds with racial cliché. In all instances, the act of imagining Africanist personae tells its own story, a story often at variance with the responses it intended to call forth.

2) The second point to be stressed is that although the language used to accommodate this Africanist persona may be overt or encoded, covert and self-reinforcing, it is also powerfully revealing. The close readings we do will decode this language. I will come back to this point about how language can sabotage or negotiate content. But first I want to put our study into historical context.

When we look at the beginnings of American literature we should remember that nineteenth-century writers were mindful of the presence of blacks; they had personal and political responses to the "problem" inherent in the contradiction of a free republic resting on and committed to a slave population. The alertness to this slave population did not confine itself to personal encounters with blacks or not. Nor to their familiarity with the publishing boom that slave narratives fed. The press, the political campaigns, the policy platforms of various parties and elected governments are rife with the slave/free discourse. It would have been an isolated individual indeed who was unaware of one of the single, if not the single, most explosive of issues in the nation. How could one speak of profit, of economy, of labor, or progress, of suffragism, or Christianity, of the frontier, of the formation of new states, the acquisition of new lands, of education, of transportation—freight and passengers—neighborhoods, quarters, the military—of practically anything a new nation concerns itself with—without having as a referent, at the heart of the discourse or defining its edges, the presence of Africans and/or their descendants? It was not possible. What did happen, frequently, was an effort to talk about these things with a vocabulary designed to disguise and displace the subject. It was not always successful, and in the work of many writers disguise was never intended. But the consequence was a master narrative (or a term I like better—white discourse) that spoke for the African and/or his descendants, and of him. Whatever popularity slave narratives had, a slave's own narrative did not destroy the master narrative, for the master narrative could accommodate many shifts, several adjustments to keep itself intact. Enforced silence from the object was needed and a kind of tacit-manipulative silence of the subject as well.

Some of the silences were broken, of course, and some maintained by authors who lived with and within the narrative. What we are interested in here are the strategies for maintaining the silence and those for breaking it. The thesis of the course is that our founding writers engaged, imagined, employed, and created an Africanistic presence and persona in several ways, and that more recent literature has followed in their footsteps.

I think we can agree that the origins of racism have been given attention for some time, as have the processes of its institutionalization, its enhancement, its denunciation, and its stubborn political usefulness. Economic and political uses and origins of notions of racial hierarchy are descriptions of part of the problem of the durability of racism, but do not address the question of why it is that even when economic and political reasons dissolve (when racist practices become not only economically unsound, but indeed begin to bankrupt a society; when the political manipulations of race backfire) racism persists. One of the explanations of this persistence is that racism is "natural" or "inevitable." That all peoples experience or share it. That it has always existed as part of human relationships. It is like saying that racism exists because black people persist in being black. Or, since physical differences among peoples do exist, those differences are there to be ranked, rather than noted—they become occasions not just of difference but also of distance.

When we look at the question of the permanence or naturalness of racism, we want to see whether its durability is linked not only to economy, politics, or speculations on class behavior, but to its metaphorical and metaphysical life that touches the marrow of American identity and therefore the core of American literature.

Obviously, in order to exploit slaves, a case had to be made for the fairness and justice of that exploitation. Rationalizing inferiority was imperative. But there may have been reasons other than material production that made racism as necessary to democracy as slavery was to slavocracy: reasons such as the accumulation of honor, dignity, power, and freedom. One of the general texts on the syllabus is Orlando Patterson's *Slavery and Social Death*. This book is a comparative study of the nature of slavery worldwide, and in it Patterson isolates some characteristics that may be useful to us in our discussions. He identifies three characteristics as integral to slave status: powerlessness, natal alienation, and dishonor. All of these terms, especially dishonor, can help us think about the persistence of racial mythology in spite of the changes in the social/economic environment that nourished it. Patterson's terms give us access to a critique of the assumptions and counter-assumptions in American literature about black peoples. If, for example, it is true that a major and universal characteristic of slave status is "social death," or "natal alienation" (which is to say that slaves were understood to have no meaningful family or social relationships, no legal or moral obligations and responsibilities to their own family members), then the enterprise of Harriet Beecher Stowe becomes radical in the mid-nineteenth century. The force of the book is not the dramatic story of escape-capture-escape, but placing, for the first time, slaves in a family context. Describing them as mothers, fathers, daughters, and so on. It is Stowe's emphasis on natal intimacy and familiarity, on social life (not social death), that made the work exceptional. One question is, What was so threatening about a slave with a history—with family obligations? Another question is, What does the deprivation of that history and family do to and for a text in which Africanisms occur?

So establishing difference and distance from some lesser dishonored "other" seems an inextricable part of the definition of nationhood (not just this one—manufacturing or resurrecting enemies is the rhetorical prerequisite in legitimate and illegitimate moves for independence), and a compelling idea in the description of an American. The characteristic urged upon the citizenry from the very beginning of the nation was difference and individualism.

Establishing difference became obsessive not only in the national character, but in the personal, domestic American character. So the question arises: Different from what? Europe, of course (this was a nation unlike corrupt, class-bound Europe). But contempt for Europe could not last through the last immigrant assimilation, or through decades of foreign affairs. It could not last for people who had come here from Europe to which they had ties and to which they returned for education, business, and, in the post–World War I era, for artistic "freedom." A major difference, therefore, could be and was found in an indigenous population that had all the characteristics necessary for sustaining the signs of difference: color. As we shall see, language and culture were suborned into this emphatic difference of color.

In addition to establishing difference, the national character was also urged and revered as "individualistic." This privileging of "individualism," the reverence for individual over collective rights, was equally forceful and the young nation was lucky in being able to develop extraordinary concepts of individuality by comparing itself to a population that was held to have contrary and opposite characteristics: collective practices, dependency, undifferentiated physical and behavioral characteristics, of being in a "fixed" place in the human and social scale, and also held to have a bound and unfree existence. These fabricated and/or stressed characteristics became serviceable marks for difference and measuring rods of individualism. The enduring legend of the cowboy figure, the Lone Ranger, is instructive here, because he is anything but alone. His credibility as solitary and powerful derives from the fact that he is accompanied by a dark-skinned serving other who functions as a willingly unfree companion. If it were not for Tonto, we would have to call him simply "Ranger." Clearly these preoccupations with race in the United States have served and continue to serve a deeply self-referential purpose, and because its purposes, its utilitarian availability is indeed self-referential, it may be that racism in its metaphysical ramifications is the most durable of all.

In dreaming race, both the subject and object of the dream are the dreamer. The literature of the United States, like its history, illustrates a movement back and forth among ideological, metaphorical, and metaphysical concepts of racial difference. But unlike history, the literature has another agenda: the private imagination acting contiguously on the external world it inhabits.

Let me return to the point of coded, but nevertheless revelatory, language. For it is the literary uses of such language that will concern us in this course.

To begin to decode the language of Africanism in American literature and to locate its specific literary uses [*stylistic tools*]—both technical strategy and structural device—we should look at the symbolic, imagistic, and conceptual sources available to these writers. Four of these are listed in the syllabus and are pertinent.

1. The so-called "meaning" of color. 2. The visual representation of blacks in Western art. 3. Patterns of Western and/or colonial thought. 4. "Scientific" racism. The distinguishing features of that part of our population who were considered definitely *not*-Americans were their slave status, their social status, and their color. It is conceivable that the first characteristic could have self-destructed earlier than it did in a variety of ways had it not been for the last: color. These slaves, unlike many others in the world's history, were visible to a fault. They were that different. And they had inherited, among other things, a centuries-and-centuries-old discourse on the "meaning" of color. It was not simply that this slave population had a distinctive color—it was that this color "meant" something, and its "meaning" had been investigated and analyzed by scholars from at least the same moment when inalienable rights were debated. One could suppose that if Africans all had three eyes, or one ear, the significance of *that* difference from the European populations would also have been found to have "meaning." In any case, much time and thought has been given to this difference in the wake of scientific explorations into categories of biology, but these were preceded by theological denotations of color and its spiritual and symbolic "meaning" during the centuries when Europe was colonizing Africa and marketing that continent's people and wealth. So by the nineteenth century ideological bias and formalistic categories in visual art could merge almost seamlessly, and a very influential book could be published in 1837 by [Frédéric] Portal on color symbolism. [See Albert Boime, *The Art of Exclusion: Representing Blacks in the Nineteenth Century*.] In this book the color black is singled out for its negative associations: "Symbol of evil and falsity, black is not a color, but rather the nega-

tion of all nuances and what they represent. Red represents divine love, but black represents infernal love, egotism, hatred and all the passions of the degraded man." Portal was not an artist nor an art historian—he was a diplomat and dilettante/historian—but his book was "rescued from oblivion" by an extremely influential art critic—[Jacques-Nicolas] Paillot de Montabert—who based his instructive manual for artists on Portal's guide. In de Montabert's manual the painter's palette is given value and meaning. "White is the symbol of Divinity of God; Black is the symbol of the evil spirit or the demon. White is the symbol of light . . . Black is the symbol of darkness and darkness expresses all evils. White is the emblem of harmony; Black is the emblem of chaos. White signifies supreme beauty; Black, ugliness. White signifies perfection; Black signifies vice. White is the symbol of innocence, Black that of guilt, sin, and moral degradation. White, a positive color, indicates happiness. Black, a negative color, indicates misfortune. The battle between good and evil is symbolically expressed by the opposition of white and black."

Where M. de Montabert got his information from, the embedded codes and overt signs of religion and ethnicity, is a subject we will take up. But it is extremely important, at this point, to note that he ascribed and distributed it as uncontested knowledge. And that it held sway in the visual arts, with many amplifications and refinements, until the present day and, as we shall see, in modern literature as well. It was not always so. And certainly it was not everywhere so. "In ancient Egypt, black signified fecundity, related to the fertilizing silt of the Nile, and this connection with the soil has also been kept in its association with death and the grave. Alchemists associated black with prime matter and latent power. The very origin of black as a pigment may be traced to the earth and its products; it was collected from the smoke of oil lamps (lamp black), from the incomplete combustion of vegetable matter (vegetable black), and from roasting the bones, horns, and ivory tusks of dead bipeds and quadrupeds (bone and ivory black). Black was associated with earth in the ancient doctrine of the four elements, considered as the basis of all material conditions (fire, air, water, and earth). Fixed relations between the four elements and their associative colors were established through the application of this scheme to the notion of the four temperaments . . . and could be interpreted as melancholy or a divine gift depending on the degree of the other 'humors.' "

Obviously "meanings" were also given to the "palette" among black African artists and sculptors prior to the triangular trade. In any case, the subjective nature of ascribing meaning to color cannot be questioned this late in the twentieth century. The significant point for this study is the alliance of "visually rendered ideas with linguistic utterances."

All peoples develop schemes for idealizing themselves, and viewing themselves as the most beautiful of all. Such views and idealizations, with their utilitarian purposes, play about in plastic images and linguistic ones and form cultural practice.

The construction of national literature as *distinctive* involved being not only not-European, it also involved being not-black. It was not only important to young America; it was and is equally important to subsequent waves of immigrants. (As a matter of fact, it wouldn't surprise me if the immigrant literature genre and experience is not determined at some point by its declaration of difference from blacks.)

"Why," asked Benjamin Franklin, "increase the sons of Africa, by planting them in America, where we have so fair an opportunity, by excluding all blacks and tawneys, of increasing the lovely white and red?" Thomas Jefferson was similarly thrilled with his own color and alarmed by black skin. "Are not the fine mixture of red and white, the expressions of every passion by greater or less suffusions of colour in the one, preferable to that eternal monotony, which reigns in the countenances, that immoveable veil of black which covers all the emotions of the other race? Add to these, flowing hair, a more elegant symmetry of form, their own judgment in favour of the whites, declared by their preferences of them, as uniformly as is the preference of the Oranootan for the black women over those of his own species."

I've gone on a bit about color and meaning, because it segues nicely into the visual images to which these writers and all of us have been subjected. Among the general and required texts is listed the Menil Foundation's giant project which culminated in four volumes edited by Hugh Honour. I hope that in the discussion groups that you will have the benefit of seeing some of the slides from this text and talking about not only the varieties of representations of blacks, but also the message within these representations and its impact on the composition itself. In a way, a look at these paintings and sketches situates us for seeing similar messages, strategies, and uses in language. The visual analogy is not, of course, limited to painting—film, illustration, commercials, theater: they all play a part. But in looking at this orderly and editorially pointed array of black and Africanistic images from antiquity to World War I, we have several points of reference. Form, color, spacial construction, design—all of the elements at play in the visual and plastic arts clarify some of the points we wish to raise.

Manet's *Olympia* is a typical example through which we can "observe how decorative oppositions of black and white, or alternative passages of light and dark, are translated into ideological statements about race and class." It is true that Manet, anxious to eliminate shadow from his painting space, hit upon an ingenious solution for achieving dramatic contrast without chiaroscuro by the interaction of the maid and the courtesan. But this in itself declares that black and white racial divisions had already been conventional in terms of the painter's palette.

Thus black and white, dark and light, were signifiers in a double sense—a dual signification still retained in the phrase "people of color." But this implies a sign in a larger linguistic system. Firstly, Manet gives us one of the fundamental aspects of the black person's status in the Western world and a type of relationship established with whites in an oppressed condition. The domestic role of the black maid shows at once that she is the custodian of Olympia's daily routine, thus freeing the courtesan for her entrepreneurial activities. If nothing else, the maid indicates the status of her mistress, which is always a notch above her own. Finally the dialectic of Manet's black and white symbolism inevitably points to the colonial enterprises of the Second Empire. The West Indian maid (identified by her head-dress) who has been induced to come to Paris for work, and has been impressed into the service of a . . . prostitute whose very existence depends upon the signs of status goes right to the heart of imperial darkness. (?) The juxtaposition of the courtesan and the exoticized black servant points inescapably to a world-embracing political system. Olympia is not only triumphant over her admiring client presenting the floral gift, but also over the colonialized "other" who mediates between them.

At the same time, Manet plays with the racial mythologies built around differences in skin color. Well aware of the purely optical character of color, Manet also knew that it carried conclusions about one's position in the social structure. A French memoir of 1777 on the security of the West Indian colonies declared that the distinction between black and white was "the principal foundation of the subordination of the slave, namely, that his *color* has made him into a slave and that nothing can make him the equal of his master." But in *Olympia* Manet reverses the traditional associations by identifying whiteness with the prostitute . . ."

It is also worthwhile to note that the ramifications of patriarchy, the license assumed with regard to the painterly explorations of the body, would make a male analogy of this painting not just shocking, as *Olympia* was, but unthinkable (or used to be unthinkable). (It took Picasso, going straight to the jugular, to do a version or revision of this famous Manet painting, by presenting Olympia alone on her couch—without a serving maid—and to render her as a black woman.) The class and gender statements are clear—even clearer are the sexual signs. Like a flag, here and especially in the literature, we see the presence of Africanism as a sign of illicit sex. It is also, as we shall see, the signification of a great deal more: power, for example, and, most especially, figurations of humaneness, compassion, and generosity.

These images of racial hierarchy exist in a very large and widely dispersed discourse that is and was the fruit of Western or European thought. Two texts, listed on the syllabus, provide some insight into the nature and consequences of this thought: Henri Baudet's *Paradise on Earth: Some Thoughts on European Images of Non-European Man* and Roberto Retamar's "Caliban."

A 1959 attempt by a Dutch historian (University of Groningen) to describe and explain an irreconcilable conflict in European thought: the desire for and veneration of Progress coupled with a yearning for a past Utopia. Baudet, writing at the nexus of post–World War II decolonialization, sees this conflict in the ways Europeans imagine non-Europeans—either savage obstacles to Western progress or residual inhabitants of Eden. The idea of progress determined the political, economic, religious, and military relationships (Baudet calls them "concrete" relationships) between Europe and "outsiders." Yet the eighteenth-century rationalism (and skepticism) did not "prevent romanticism, sentiment and exoticism" from influencing Europe's relations with the "outside world." [p. 54] The domain of the European imagination, however—"images and symbols formed of non-Western peoples" [vii]—disregards the fact of observation/experience, etc., and is a "psychological urge." These antithetic tendencies result in an ambivalence that monitors regression and expansion/aggression. Regression, based on principles of "Christian charity," produces both the "noble savage" and expansionism. The *dualism* ("double consciousness" of which W. E. B. Dubois spoke) is therefore not limited to the debates of non-Europeans (i.e., Achebe, Soyinka, etc.), but is here a central facet of Western perception.

Baudet's essay may be seriously flawed by his own romanticism:

the construction of "simple, good natives in a cultureless environment." This latter being understood by him to be the original "home" of Europe since (a) the birth of Europe from Cap d'Asie (outpost of Africa) to world leader encourages such nostalgia, and (b) Christianity charts the expulsion from this "home" (Eden) as a "fall."

What may be lacking in his argument is a more persuasive explanation of the nasty turn exoticism takes: what surfaces is not only *le bon negre* or the "noble savage" but also *le sol negre* and the savage beast deserving/requiring conquest and extermination. This latter becomes a cold expansionism and exploitation, that Baudet locates in Europe's early history as an "area of invasion"—attached on all sides by Turks, Muslims, etc., and political expediency. This "concrete" political world he implies is separate from the "imaginative, symbolical" one; and only the latter is the subject of the essay. He notes the change in the European perception of Paradise/Eden as a change from Eden in *time* (the revered ancestral past), to Eden in *space* (the urge to geographic conquest), to the modern Eden as *now* (universalist, socialist and anti-historical . . .).

In III Baudet has interesting things to say about the evolution of history. Where nineteenth-century history abandoned the mythological and universalist philosophic underpinnings of the eighteenth century (when "history" was in fact the reflections of philosophers on universalist themes) to *develop history as nationalism*—a move Baudet suggests (after Burkhardt) is the birth of World History—in spite of the fact that the "world" historicized was Eurocentric. World history could regard "l'peuple" (read "masses") as its internal barbarians, having no need for foreign or exotic barbarians as did the earlier century.

[Ernest] Renan's [?] *Tempest* underscores, for him, the modern dilemma: the "people" look to and merge with Caliban (now heavily influenced by Europe) in contesting and overthrowing Prospero. The "people/masses" *and* Caliban become the proletarian, both urging a (socialist) promise of a golden future.

These discursive attitudes and quasi-historical concepts of the existence and the inevitability of racial "othering" are bolstered with "scientific" racism. The scientific community's efforts to document and explain the biological inferiority of blacks. From the eleventh edition of the Encyclopedia's description of the deficiency of black people's brains, to whole batteries of mis-applied and mis-interpreted intelligence tests, to the anatomy experiments that Stephen Jay Gould replicated and proved false, to more casual but no less ludicrous summations of everyday scientific scholars and laymen. Among the interesting phenomena in much of the written work the scientific community has produced (and it is important to remember the impact of eighteenth- and nineteenth-century interest in man's evolution) is the powerfully suggestive, even voluptuous, language used.

Sander Gilman, in *On Blackness Without Blacks,* quotes several of these, and one I'd like to read. As I do, notice the metaphoric language in which the argument is expressed.

According to unalterable physiological laws, negroes, as a general rule, to which there are but few exceptions, can only have their intellectual faculties awakened in a sufficient degree to receive moral culture, and to profit by religious or other instruction, when under the compulsatory authority of the white man; because, as a general rule, to which there are but few exceptions, they will not take sufficient exercise, when removed from the white man's authority, to vitalize and decarbonize their blood by the process of full and free respiration, that active exercise of some kind alone can effect. A northern climate remedies, in a considerable degree, their naturally indolent disposition; but the dense atmosphere of Boston or Canada can scarcely produce sufficient hematosis and vigor of mind to induce them to labor. From their natural indolence, unless under the stimulus of compulsion, they doze away their lives with the capacity of their lungs for atmospheric air only half expanded, from the want of exercise to superinduce full and deep respiration. The inevitable effect is, to prevent a sufficient atmospherization or vitalization of the blood, so essential to the expansion and the freedom of action of the intellectual faculties. The *black blood* distributed to the brain *chains* the mind to ignorance, superstition and barbarism, and *bolts the door* against civilization, moral culture and religious truth. The *compulsory power* of the white man, by making the slothful negro take active exercise, puts into active play the lungs, through whose agency the vitalized blood is sent to the brain to give *liberty* to the mind, and to *open the door* to intellectual improvement. The very exercise, so beneficial to the negro, is expended in cultivating those burning fields in cotton, sugar, rice and tobacco which, but for his labor, would, from the heat of the climate, go uncultivated, and their products lost to the world. Both parties are benefitted—the negro as well as his master—even more. *But there is a third party benefitted—the world at large. The three millions of bales of cotton, made by negro labor, afford a cheap clothing for the civilized world. The laboring classes of all mankind, having less to pay for clothing, have more money to spend in educating their children, and in intellectual, moral and religious progress.*

The wisdom, mercy, and justice of the decree, that Canaan shall serve Japheth, is proved by the disease we have been considering, because it proves that his physical organization, and the laws of his nature, are in perfect unison with slavery, and in entire discordance with liberty—a discordance so great as to produce the loathsome disease that we have been considering, as one of its inevitable effects—a disease that locks up the understanding, blunts the sensations, and chains the mind to superstition, ignorance, and barbarism. Slaves are not subject to this disease, unless they are permitted to live like free negroes, in idleness and filth—to eat improper food, or to indulge in spirituous liquors.

That is a splendid example of what Aldon Nielsen would call "white discourse." His book *Reading Race: White American Poets and the Racial Discourse in the Twentieth Century* consists of close readings of poetry, but the introduction is valuable because in it he discusses fiction: Melville's *White-Jacket* and *Benito Cereno* and Gertrude Stein's "Melanctha."

His inquiry is into how writers' racial attitudes are reflected in their work. He refers to the construction of "white discourse," seeing it as a veil separating the races and enforcing white power. His support includes [Mikhail] Bakhtin—whom he quotes for the observation that "the intention of the representing discourse is at odds with represented discourse"—and Frank Lentricchia, among others. "Because language inhabits all its speakers, its representations come to seem universal laws; they acquire that naturalness of which Lentricchia speaks. That arrival at naturalness is indicative of the maturity of the representation. Like a frozen or dead metaphor, it no longer requires explanation among native speakers." It is "the mark of the stable 'mature' society whose ideological apparatus is so deeply set in place, so well buried, so unexamined a basis of our judgment and feeling that it is taken for truth with a capital letter."

Although Nielsen touches upon the construction of this "white" discourse, his study confines itself to ways in which stereotypes are distributed in writers' work. His inquiry does not extend to [ours]— how imaginative encounters with and employment of racial codes illuminate the work and the writers' self-meditation—a meditation that may not be about race at all, but about strategies for self-reflection. That is, an examination of the surrogacy, the exploitation, and the serviceability of Africanism may lead us to regard the linguistic veil not as a screen (impenetrable, translucent, or transparent) but as a mirror, insomuch as it (this discourse) seems to reflect areas of self-meditation and self-regard and is not merely "self-enforcing."

For example, if one takes the famous Stein quote that Nielsen uses here to good purpose ("the negroes were not suffering from persecution; they were suffering from nothingness," and "needless are niggers" ["Dinner" in *Tender Buttons*]) and allies it with the fear of "historylessness" of new America; its rejection of a corrupt European past; its desire to be both new and innocent, and the attendant dread such contextlessness brings, the quote becomes a useful index into the complex problem of forming "identity" out of nothing. To Stein, negro aesthetics, that is, African sculpture/art, is sophisticated, but narrow and ancient suggests the powerful presence of "history" (ancientness) she sees in it. How does that "ancientness" become "nothingness"? Nielsen points up these contradictions, but does not examine how they sabotage the veil, the screen and become luminous moments of self-revelation—not about power, but about vulnerability.

The final items I want to touch upon are four topics that will serve as a method of inquiry.

The surrogate self as enabler.
The employment of an Africanistic idiom.
The function of Africanist character.
The utilization of an Africanist narrative.

The Surrogate Self as Enabler

This phrase calls our attention to two aspects of Africanism: (1) the way Africanistic presences enable the author/narrator to make certain explorations, and (2) the way such a presence enables the text.

For the first concern or focus, we will think of these imagined Africans and African-American fictional characters as substitute or surrogate versions of the self. Not as *extensions* of the self, but as *forms* of the self—an estranged self—that can be explored, ignored, or embraced depending upon what problems and interests the narrator/author put on display. For example, if Edgar Allan Poe is interested in madness as ratiocination, as excessive genius, he draws upon white male characters. When he wishes to illuminate madness as irrational, comic, ludicrous, he examines it in a woman (Zenobia) or in a lunatic, defective black man. When problems of fear, impotence, loss of status, or power or freedom surface in the text, a surrogate Africanistic figure is frequently introduced to provide a terrain for this examination, a safe terrain, since focusing on a discredited "other" can protect the narrative voice from a too-explosive self-examination, project into terrain it considers foreign, alien to its own.

The second aspect (how an Africanistic presence enables the text) requires us to locate instances in which the work, the book, is helped along, how the plot is oiled, how the next narrative move is made, how transitions are facilitated, how the news is brought, and so on by a readily and always available Africanistic presence to do the work. Jupiter the slave and manservant in "The Goldbug" is such an enabler—the one who voices alarm, who provides the dread, who seeks the narrator's help when his master seems to be in great difficulty, and who is instrumental in securing the treasure. It is interesting, however, to note that Jupiter is quickly dismissed from the plot altogether at the moment when sharing . . .

In *Moby-Dick,* Queequeg enables the "I" of the tale, Ishmael, to select the ship (actually it is Queequeg's "negro idol" which directs them). This black man, this Africanistic figure, is also the one who initiates Ishmael into the world of whaling as well as provides Ishmael the means for his (Ishmael's) solitary and singular survival.

In modern fiction, the gesture does not require elaboration. In Flannery O'Connor, in William Styron's work an Africanistic figure can simply walk onstage, as it were, and walk right off, and the signals are clear. Signals of unbridled sexuality, of limitless love, of violence, of nurture—whatever the author wishes to pick from the collection of stereotypical views, attitudes, assumptions—we are calling Africanism.

The next strategic use of Africanism is the *employment of an Africanistic idiom:* a degraded language; an awkward silencing; a prophetic articulation. The first, degraded, estranged language has been the most popular. [*Concept of Black languages as sophisticated/hip is recent and a sign of its modernity.*] Like any new country, colonial and post-colonial America was developing its own language, its own literariness. Debating the inclusion of the language of common people and colloquial uses—lauding them as in Mark Twain's work or resisting them as in Henry James's—welcoming or scorning dialect in fiction. [*Great vogue of dialect.*] The speech, the dialogue of Africans and African-Americans, however, had an additional agenda in literature.

Writers found it necessary to clarify the difference between the speech of white Americans and the speech of African-Americans—a speech difference that did not follow the lines of every other merging of speech habits, but one that resisted all efforts to belong to American language. Or seemed to. We have to ask ourselves what is the point not only of Poe's efforts at establishing language difference, but also of Harriet Beecher Stowe's similar efforts in *Uncle Tom's Cabin*. For the difference they are at pains to show is not just other; it is also lesser. When you reread "The Goldbug," pay particular attention to anomalies in his rendering of so-called "black" dialect. [*Orthography*] For example, when he has Jupiter say "I knows it," he spells "knows" n-o-s-e: the spelling and phonetic alteration are at odds.

Africanistic idiom is the rendering of this Black speech, dialogue, and the authorial comments on this dialogue, and the response such renderings are designed to elicit from readers. This idiom serves several purposes. One is the effort to distance one's self from the dark other and to privilege one's own language or dialect. It can be done in the ways Poe does it, by mis-spelling and deliberate mis-rendering of speech. It can also be done as Hemingway does upon occasion by giving a black character the specific language of dishonor and cowardice as in *To Have and Have Not*, even when it risks structural coherence within the text. But this same use of Africanistic idiom can also be the terse eloquence of certain Africanistic Faulknerian characters as well as their significant silences, offering comparison with his excessively verbal white figures. The speech of Sam Fathers, for example, in "The Bear," is rendered with these silences. Giving him a pre-racial, Edenesque profundity. And it is worthwhile to note when and why the locus of a work in which blacks are central, in which what they say is important, or is to be taken seriously, takes place outside time or far away from civilization: the sea, the forest, the territory. And the question becomes how and why this isolation from urban or "civilized" locations makes undegraded and undifferentiated black speech possible.

In addition to estranging and disfamiliarizing black speech, there are five other linguistic techniques which help in the construction of a mythic but serviceable Africanistic other: [You may want to write these down because we will return to them time and time again.]

1) *fetishizing strategies*—the blood fetish being the most powerful (black blood, polluted blood, "mixed" blood; half-"breed," etc.);

2) *metonymic displacement or reduction*—the use of color, black, to call up large and conclusive prejudices; to stand in for all the varieties of an individual personality;

3) *the economy of stereotype*—using labels such as "nigger" relieves the writer from any responsibility to describe a character fully; it becomes a shortcut as well as a dismissal when Hemingway says "the nigger said" or "we had this nigger." The assumption is that the reader needs no further information;

4) *use of metaphors and similes* (a) *metaphors which collapse humans into animals*—a recourse to bestial or animalistic comparisons is rife throughout the literature. Overwhelming in Poe: Pompey in "How to Write a Blackwood Article," *The Narrative of A. Gordon Pym* [the Dirk Peters character], "Murders in the Rue Morgue" and the Ourang-Outang that is the culprit; (b) *metaphoric condensation*—in which an Africanistic persona *equals* sensuality, irrationality, evil, anarchy.

5) *allegory and allegorical mechanisms*—in some instances such as in *Moby-Dick*, allegory discloses deeper interpretations; in others allegory is used deliberately to foreclose discussion.

When these techniques are not available or when they are jettisoned, there is a kind of textual tremor when authors both reveal and conceal relationships between whites and blacks that are intimate:

non sequitur in Poe; disjunctive and disjointed texts in Faulkner and Styron; gaps, evasions, disruptions and violent contradictions and lapses. (For example, why is Jupiter permitted, assigned the role of whipping Le Grand, his master?)

The third focus is on the *function of Africanist characters*—not as surrogate selves, but as guides, as markers and delineations of white character. Here we will look at the ways black characters are used to comment on the qualities and characteristics of non-black people. Our readerly feelings about a character, a white character, are oftentimes guided by that character's relationship to a black one. We can trust Ishmael, like him, join him, emotionally, *because* he makes himself available to, and open to, liking the savage Queequeg. The moral dilemma of Huckleberry Finn, passed on to him by "respectable" society, is resolved by his fraternal relationship with the black slave Jim. If Huck had been in the company of a white escaping convict, his final act of loyalty, of risking hell rather than turn his companion over, would not have had the same weight it has now in the text. No other companionship, certainly in the mid-nineteenth century—would have given Huck the moral purpose and superiority to the so-called respectable people the way his commitment to a slave does. Breaking the law for an African, thinking of this distanced person as a friend worth risking something for, puts Huck on the high ground morally and gives him the *freedom* and the humanism the text hinges on. (Huck's freedom is *dependent* on a slave.)

Gertrude Stein comments substantially on white feminine sexuality and oppression by her insertion of Melanctha's story between the two white, immigrant servants in *Three Lives*. When Hemingway wants his readers to understand how virile, how expert, how compassionate Harry is, he uses Africanistic characters as marks of delineation.

Sometimes the functions of these characters are a means of exploring the body: in the guise of sexuality, vulnerability, a kind of presumed anarchy or chaos projected onto black characters to signify the opposite of or the threat to white characters. What are the implications of pleasure, of domination, of freedom in references to the body when the body in question is black? Flannery O'Connor's story, *Uncle Tom's Cabin,* William Styron, and others indicate the generosity, largesse, the discipline, the virility, the virtue, the status of whites by juxtaposing them to Africanistic characters.

The final area concerns *Africanistic narrative:* the telling of a black story. Generally, this kind of narrative is about blacks, or from the point of view of a black, or contains central characters who are black. It can also be a narrative that employs black or Africanistic signs and formula. Stowe's *Uncle Tom's Cabin,* William Styron's *Nat Turner,* Willa Cather's *Sapphira and the Slave Girl,* and Bellow's *Henderson the Rain King* are among the books that fall into this category.

In these narratives we will note whether there are degrees of blackness and what being more or less black means to the narrative voice. What is the voice being empathetic or hostile to? What is assumed to be the desire or preference of the speaking blacks? Does the preference reinforce the authorial voice, and when does it defy it, contradict or sabotage it? What is the consequence of the black character's presence to the narrative? What is narratively possible when and after the character appears?

Edgar Allan Poe/Herman Melville

In *The Narrative of A. Gordon Pym,* Edgar Allan Poe describes the culmination of an extraordinary journey.

March 21st—A sullen darkness now hovered above us—but from out the milky depths of the ocean a luminous glare arose, and stole up along the bulwarks of the boat. We were nearly overwhelmed by the white ashy shower which settled upon us and upon the canoe, but melted into the water as it fell.

March 22nd.—The darkness had materially increased, relieved only by the glare of the water thrown back from the white curtin [*sic*] before us. Many gigantic and pallidly white birds flew continuously now from beyond the veil, and their scream was the eternal Tekeli-li! as they retreated from our vision. Hereupon Nu-Nu stirred in the bottom of the boat; but upon touching him, we found his spirit departed. And now we rushed into the embraces of the cataract, where a chasm threw itself open to receive us. But there arose in our pathway a shrouded human figure, very far larger in its proportions than any dweller among men. And the hue of the skin of the figure was of the perfect whiteness of the snow.

They have been floating, Pym and Peter and the native Nu-Nu, upon a warm, milk-white sea under showers of "a fine white powder"; the black man, Nu-Nu, is now dead, and they rush forward through the white curtain to a large white giant. After that, there is nothing. Footnotes, explanations, and a highly interesting conclusion among the notes into which the narrative drifts: that it was whiteness that terrified the "affrighted natives," and that carved into the walls of the cliffs they passed through was this quotation: "I have graven it within the hills, and my vengeance upon the dust within the rock."

Those two comments in the final notes replicate the dilemma of Young America: *first,* the constitution of a whiteness that is capable, by virtue of its assumption and position of power, of "affright[ing]" the natives. It is understood by Poe and his generation of American writers—this inherent power and threat of the *color* white; *second,* a message, engraved, inscribed, eternalized on the very earth itself: a warning of vengeance, alarming and terrifying.

Rocking back and forth between the two comments is the dilemma: constructing a powerful, dominating, exclusionary whiteness that worries about the possibility of retribution and vengeance for having done so.

Furthermore, Poe's *Narrative* contains a salient image that is instructive for our investigation of Africanist discourse in general and early American literature in particular. This final journey is within whiteness, on whiteness, toward whiteness. An impenetrable whiteness the figure of which is the obstruction of a veil, a curtain. When the black native dies, and there is just Pym and Peter, his Africanist companion, the final obstacles surface—a chasm into which they are about to fall and a huge shrouded human figure whose skin is "the perfect whiteness of the snow."

Are they saved by the white figure? Saved from the chasm? Or is the white figure more threatening, more terrifying than the cataract? Why "shrouded"? Is "shrouded" meant to echo and stress the white curtain that blinds and obstructs their journey? All of these meanings come into play, heightened by the ambivalence and ambiguity on display here about whiteness, blackness, and a variety of Africanist images characterizing early American literature.

No early American writer is more suggestive of the matters under review in this course than Edgar Allan Poe. Darling of the French symbolist poets, favorite of anthologizers, taught to young readers, perused by literary scholars, acknowledged as a genius by writers as powerful and dissimilar as Henry James and Dostoyevsky, and a familiar, popular writer to every generation of Americans since the nineteenth century. Journalist, literary critic, poet, short story writer, and novelist, Poe touches almost every form available to writers of his time, and exceeds most in the variety of genres worked in and the stretch of his imagination. His life, not less than his work, encourages literary immortality. He was orphaned, alienated, romantic, morbid, alcoholic, intellectual, tragic, and he died young. Also he romanticized girls, love, and death, was white, male, and classically racist.

Let's examine the latter three. Poe contributed to and promulgated a specific and detested, imagined and wholly fabricated Africanistic presence: a kind of black thing—not quite human, not quite not, but available for all sorts of labor, all sorts of sport, all sorts of fantasy and many sorts of transfer. This Africanist presence hovers at the margins of Poe's texts when it does not inform them directly, and although (if not because) the presence is black, it throws considerable light on the work. Principal among the signs of this hovering presence are Poe's own horror of black as a color and his love of it; his sometimes amused, sometimes impatient, sometimes raging contempt for blacks as people and his fear of them; his attempts to distance them in language and gesture from the human race; his dependence on them as surrogates for his ambivalence about his own social status and inheritance; one easily senses his identification with and terror of the solitude and dishonor of Africanism; his sensitivity to the struggle of the artist in a crude, uncivilized Philistine world; his fascination with soil, earth, caves, the grave, the underground, and all of the other connotative and associative meanings of blackness as well as the fearfulness of darkness and the impenetrableness [impenetrability] of whiteness.

Some of our attention will be directed to this configuration and figuration of what is hidden behind and within the assumptions of a culturally formed whiteness, how dependent and inextricably bound that formation is with Africanism. How Poe's milky-white shroud comes into existence, as it does in Pym's journey, after and only after an encounter with a black or Africanistic world; how the dread of the consequences of that encounter is not only inscribed on the very rocks and cliffs of the earth for Pym, but also is inscribed through much of American literature; how pathologically provocative, or brilliantly stimulating, how deeply passionate the encounter with Africanism is, and how the excesses of that response lead to the absence of knowledge, to self-sabotaging work, and the non sequitur that is the final utterance of *The Narrative of A. Gordon Pym*.

Just as certain imaginatively mature and open responses to Africanism lead to clarity, artistic liberation in some cases, when the writer is "freed up" to contest these assumptions, he or she problematizes/complicates the encounter and lets us see the mechanics of that problematization. The works of Herman Melville add a great deal to that level of discourse: choosing to complicate rather than simplify.

But before discussing Melville briefly, I want to turn your attention to some of the details of the enterprise in which writers in Young America were engaged. I mentioned last week that at the heart of the American enterprise was the construction of a new, white male.

The literature, fiction, poetry, essays, journalism—all attest to the urgency of this moment and the creature capable of seizing it. There is a paradigm for this construction in an extraordinary book by Bernard Bailyn, called *Voyagers to the West: A Passage in the Peopling of America on the Eve of the Revolution*. I want to quote a rather long passage from that book because it helps to clarify and underscore the salient aspects of this American character that I have been describing:

> William Dunbar, seen through his letters and diary, appears to be more fictional than real—a creature of William Faulkner's imagination, a more cultivated Colonel Sutpen but no less mysterious. He, too, like that strange character in *Absalom, Absalom!*, was a man in his early twenties who appeared suddenly in the Mississippi wilderness to stake out a claim to a large parcel of land, then disappeared to the Caribbean to return leading a battalion of "wild" slaves with whose labor alone he built an estate where before there had been nothing but trees and uncultivated soil. But he was more complex than Sutpen, if no less driving in his early ambitions, no less a progenitor of a notable Southern family, and no less a part of a violent biracial world whose tensions could lead in strange directions. For this wilderness planter was a scientist, who would later correspond with Jefferson on science and exploration. A Mississippi planter whose contributions to the American Philosophical Society (to which Jefferson proposed him for membership) included linguistics, archeology, hydrostatics, astronomy, and climatology, and whose geographical explorations were reported in widely known publications. Like Sutpen an exotic figure in the plantation world of early Mississippi—Dunbar was known as "Sir" William just as Sutpen was known as "Colonel"—he too imported into that raw, half-savage world the niceties of European culture: not chandeliers and costly rugs, but books, surveyor's equipment of the finest kind, and the latest instruments of science.

Dunbar was a Scot by birth, the youngest son of Sir Archibald Dunbar of Morayshire. He was educated first by tutors at home, then at the university in Aberdeen, where his interest in mathematics, astronomy, and belles lettres took mature shape. What happened to him after his return home and later in London, where he circulated with young intellectuals, what propelled, or led, him out of the metropolis on the first leg of his long voyage west is not known. But whatever his motivation may have been, in April 1771, aged only twenty-two, Dunbar appeared in Philadelphia. . . .

Ever eager for gentility, this well-educated product of the Scottish enlightenment and of London's sophistication—this bookish young litterateur and scientist, who, only five years earlier, had been corresponding about scientific problems—about "Dean Swift's beatitudes," about the "virtuous and happy life," and about the Lord's commandment that mankind should "love one another"— was strangely insensitive to the suffering of those who served him. In July 1776, he recorded not the independence of the American colonies from Britain, but the suppression of an alleged conspiracy for freedom by slaves on his own plantation. . . .

Dunbar, the young erudite, the Scottish scientist and man of letters, was no sadist. His plantation regime was, by the standards of the time, mild; he clothed and fed his slaves decently, and frequently relented in his more severe punishments. But, 4,000 miles from the sources of culture, alone on the far periphery of British civilization where physical survival was a daily struggle, where ruthless exploitation was a way of life, and where disorder, violence, and human degradation were commonplace, he had triumphed by successful adaptation. Endlessly enterprising and resourceful, his finer sensibilities dulled by the abrasions of frontier life, and feeling within himself a sense of authority and autonomy he had not known before, a force that flowed from his absolute control over the lives of others, he emerged a distinctive new man, a borderland gentleman, a man of property in a raw, half-savage world.

May I call your attention to some elements of this portrait; some pairings and interdependencies that are marked in this narrative of William Dunbar? First, the historical connection between the Enlightenment and the institution of slavery—the rights of man and his enslavement. Second, the relationship of Dunbar's education and his new world enterprise. The education he had was exceptional and exceptionally cultivated: it included the latest thought on theology and science—an effort perhaps to make them mutually accountable, to make each support the other. He is not only the "product of the Scottish enlightenment," he is the consequence of "London sophistication." He read Swift, discussed the Christian commandment to "love one another," and is described as "strangely" insensitive to the suffering of his slaves. On July 12, 1776, he is recording with astonishment and hurt surprise the slave rebellion on his plantation. "Judge my surprise . . . ," he wrote. "Of what avail is kindness and good usage when rewarded by such ingratitude." "Constantly bewildered," Bailyn goes on, "by his slaves behavior, [Dunbar] recovered two runaways and condemned them to receive 500 lashes each at five different times, and to carry a chain and log fixt to the ancle [*sic*]." I take this to be a succinct portrait of the process by which the American as new, white, and male was constituted. It is a formation which has at least four desirable consequences, all of which are referred to in Bailyn's summation of Dunbar's character and located in how Dunbar feels "within himself." Let me repeat: "a sense of authority and autonomy he had not known before, a force that flowed from his absolute control over the lives of others, he emerged a distinctive new man, a borderland gentleman, a man of property in a raw, half-savage world." A power, a sense of freedom he had not known before. But what had he "known before"? Fine education, London sophistication, theological and scientific thought. None of these, one gathers, could provide him with the authority and autonomy Mississippi planter life did. Also this "sense" is understood to be a "force" that "flows," already present and ready to spill as a result of his "absolute control over the lives of others." This "force" is not a willed domination here, a thought-out, calculated choice, but rather a kind of natural resource, a Niagara Falls waiting to drench Dunbar as soon as he is in a position to possess absolute control over others. And once he has moved into that position, he is resurrected as a new man, a distinctive man—a different man. Also, whatever his social status in London, in the New World he is a gentle man. More gentle. More man. Because the site of his transformation is within rawness. He is backgrounded by savagery.

I want to suggest that these concerns—autonomy, authority, newness and difference, and absolute power—not only become the major themes and presumptions of American literature, but that each one is made possible by, shaped by, activated by a complex awareness and employment of a constituted Africanism. I want to suggest that it was this Africanism, deployed as rawness and savagery, that provided the staging ground and arena for the elaboration of that quintessential American identity.

Autonomy is freedom and translates into the much championed and revered "individualism"; newness translates into "innocence"; distinctiveness becomes difference and the erection of strategies for maintaining it; authority and absolute power become a romantic, conquering "heroism," "virility," and the problematics of wielding absolute power over the lives of others. All the rest are made possible by this last, it would seem—absolute power called forth and acted out, against, upon, and within a natural and mental landscape conceived of as a "raw, half-savage world."

Why is it seen as "raw and savage"? Because it is peopled by a non-white indigenous population? Perhaps. But certainly because there is readily to hand a bound and unfree, rebellious but serviceable black population by which Dunbar and all whitemen are enabled to measure these privileging and privileged differences.

Eventually individualism will fuse with the prototype of Americans as solitary, alienated, malcontent. What are Americans always so insistently innocent of? Different from? And as for absolute power, over whom is this power held, from whom withheld, to whom distributed?

Answers to these questions lie in the potent and ego-reinforcing presence of an Africanistic population. This population is convenient in every way, not the least of which is self-definition. This new white male can now persuade himself that savagery is "out there." That the lashes ordered (500 applied 5 times is 2,500) are not one's own savagery; that repeated and dangerous breaks for freedom are "puzzling" confirmations of black irrationality; that the combination of Dean Swift's beatitudes and a life of regularized violence is civilized; that, if the sensibilities are dulled enough, the rawness remains external.

These contradictions cut and slash their way through the pages of American literature.

Bailyn's description is a cameo of the *Construction of the American as white and male.*

1. PRODUCT OF THE SCOTTISH ENLIGHTENMENT.
   Underscores the relationship between the Age of
   Enlightenment and the Age of Racism. Both concepts born
   at the same time. Perhaps, in its inquisition into *freedom*
   (the rights of man) and *reason* there would need to be the
   dramatization of these ideas with their opposites.
2. AUTHORITY 3. AUTONOMY 4. NEWNESS
   Authority comes from this so-called "force" that "flowed"
   from absolute control over the lives of others. Slavery, then,
   becomes an absolute necessity, as does the control over the
   lives of women.
   Autonomy is license and individuality, an irrepressible theme
   in American letters.
   Newness, what Bailyn called a "distinctive new man,"
   becomes willful refusal of history. What Irving Howe calls a
   "first principle."
5. DIFFERENCE WITHIN A RAW, HALF-SAVAGE
   WORLD is a view that relegates the surrounding and
   inhabiting peoples as alien, unreasoning, and uncivilized.

A close look at these terms used to describe Dunbar (enlightenment, background, authority, autonomy, newness, and a "civilized" difference from environment) reveals that they are all features he (Dunbar) *had not known before.*

Before we look at the defining terms of this originizing American, we should look at what he *had* known before.

WHAT HE HAD NOT KNOWN BEFORE

The habit of genuflection would be replaced by the thrill of command, power, control of one's own destiny instead of the powerlessness that the unemployed, the dispossessed, the abused laborers, farmers, craftsmen, petty thieves, social and family outcasts had felt before the gates of class, caste, and cunning persecution. In other words, one could move from being disciplined and punished to disciplining and punishing; from social ostracism to becoming arbiters of social strata; from a useless, binding, repulsive past into a kind of historylessness—a blank page waiting to be inscribed. Much was to be written in that shadow: noble impulses were made into law and tradition; base ones, learned and appropriated in the rejected and rejecting homeland, were also made into law and tradition.

(1) DUNBAR, PRODUCT OF THE SCOTTISH ENLIGHTENMENT

Age of Enlightenment/Age of Reason

This shockingly attractive idea of the "rights of man" being God-given, inalienable, was allied with another idea—the hierarchy of race. Orlando Patterson has suggested that we should not be surprised that the Enlightenment accompanied slavery in this country; we should be surprised if it did not; if the concept of freedom emerged in a vacuum. As it was, nothing highlighted freedom, if it did not, in fact, create it, like slavery. And black slavery simply made the creative possibilities more theatrical. (Jefferson) For in that construction one finds not only the not-free, but also, due to the color of skin, the not-me. The result was a kind of playground for the imagination, and what rose up in the collective imagination was a fabrication of darkness, otherness, fear, and desire—that is uniquely American, unlike, in many respects, European Africanism (which has its counterpart in its own colonial literature).

> The dogma of the inferiority of the Negro begins largely with the beginnings of the Age of Reason in the eighteenth century and has been reinforced from all sources since. A corollary dogma which arose almost simultaneously stated that slavery was the ideal state for such inferior and inadequate persons and indeed that freedom resulted in their decay and degradation. The nineteenth century political, sociological and anthropological literature is filled with the demonstration of these allegations.
>
> Pasamanick's understanding of the special relationship created between blackness and madness reflects the growing politicization of the concept of Blackness in the late 18th and 19th centuries. For as the concept of "Black" and the concept of "Slave" merged, special criteria were evolved for dealing with the special status of the Black as slave in Western consciousness. He became either the noble enslaved prince or the marginal man saved from barbarity by civilization. This alteration in perspective incorporated the existing model of the nexus between madness and blackness to achieve its varied ends.

The image that informs much of Emerson's writing in the 1830s is that of an early America, still the infant republic of independent farmers and craftsmen, still largely egalitarian in tone and, to a lesser degree, social content, still vibrating to the memory of the revolution. Half a century later Henry Adams would write:

Except for Negro slavery, [early-nineteenth-century America] was sound and healthy in every part. Stripped for the hardest work, every muscle firm and elastic, every ounce of brain ready for use, and not a trace of superfluous flesh on his nervous and supple body, the American stood in the world as a new order.

(2) AUTHORITY

In her perceptive analysis of the American character, Constance Rourke notes *the tendency of American legendary characters to be over-blown, exaggerated figures and points out that this ideal image of the self is often the result of anxiety and self-doubt.* The American legendary character, writes Rourke, was *obsessed with strength and triumph and "seemed obliged to shout their symbols as if after all he were not wholly secure in their possession."* "The Yankee and the backwoodsman, for example, were ideal figures participating in a masquerade, and the qualities they adopted were designed to give them confidence and self-esteem."

When the image of the individual is disproportionately large, there is no room for the individuality of other people. The individual who is so intent on establishing his own persona cannot look outward. Thus, as Constance Rourke also observes, American legendary characters were all solitary male figures, without wife, family, or any other human relationships: "They appeared always as single figures, or merely doubled and multiplied, never as one of a natural group, never as part of a complex human situation, always nomadic." These legendary characters became "emblems of the national life." The "American Narcissus," says Rourke, looked at himself in this unreal, inflated, isolated figure and saw what he wanted to see—an ideal picture of himself.

Individualism and the Other

Like Indians and blacks in nineteenth-century America, women as a group were excluded from participation in the American Dream.

The nineteenth-century individualist was white, and he was a man. The American cultural ideal has been the unencumbered expanding white male individualist. However illusory the promise of America may have proved to be for many men, the dominant image for the white American male was that of a larger-than-life superhero whose world was wrought for himself and by himself. (Joyce Warren)

(3) AUTONOMY

Autonomy, of course, translates as "individualism," for Hawthorne, Thoreau, Melville, Cooper, and especially Emerson:

I) Joyce W. Warren, The American Narcissus

"After detailing the virtues of the strong individual, he [Emerson] uses the example of the real estate entrepreneur, thus making very American his exemplary man: 'A feeble man can see the farms that are fenced and tilled, the houses that are built. The strong man sees the possible house and farms. His eye makes estates as fast as the sun breeds clouds.'"

Further examples in "Uses of Great Men, 1845" are those who stand above the masses—railroad builders, "a great salesman, then a road-contractor, then a student of fishes." All nineteenth-century images of success and American ideas of the necessity for wealth and power.

"Of the California gold rush, for example, he wrote that it did not matter what immoral means were used: the function of the gold rush was to hasten the settlement and *civilizing* of the West."

II) On Thoreau

"Relationships with others were a waste of time; they threatened the integrity of the self and interfered with the expansion of the individual soul . . ."

"What he wanted in a friend was the confirmation of the self."

"This inability, or unwillingness, to put himself in another's place was the result of a self-absorption that negated the significance of other people."

III) Irving Howe, The American Newness

"Hawthorne's best short fictions deal with the costs of the isolated self; nothing in Emerson's journals is more poignant than his repeated self-excoriation for failing to show sufficient warmth to friends. *The burden of isolation is of course a central theme in American literature:* Hawthorne copes with it through the closing of small human circles; Emerson, through invocations of selfhood grounded in a spiritualized nature. What links these seemingly distant writers, transcending their clashes of opinion, is a devotion to *inwardness,* a risky, powerful mode of personal existence that, in its nineteenth-century romantic forms, is just starting to undergo historical test."

IV) Joyce Warren, The American Narcissus: Individualism and Women in 19th-Century American Fiction

"*Americans took the concept of individualism*—in Europe, a negative concept connoting selfishness and social anarchy—*and transformed it so that it not only came to represent the positive qualities of freedom and self-determination but actually became synonymous with American-ism and the proudly proclaimed 'American way of life.'* In this respect American republicanism differed from democratic tendencies in other countries, where the emphasis was on collectivism and social unity rather than on individual rights. In European democracies, sovereignty remained in the state; in America, sovereignty rested instead in the individual. Individualism became a peculiar characteristic of American life. All of America's institutions are an expression of individualism; all of its major political parties have made individualism part of their platforms; the philosophies and religions developed in America were based in individualism; and even most reform movements in America have been individualistic in their aims."

(4) NEWNESS

Whatever the reasons, the attraction was of the "clean slate" variety—a kind of unprecedented opportunity not only to be born again, but to be born again in new clothes, as it were, raiment provided by the new place in which this re-birth could take place. Moreover, it was to have a second chance that could benefit from the mistakes of a first one. There must have been the gleaming aspect of a limitless future, made more gleaming by the dissatisfaction and turmoil being left behind. The promise was genuinely promising. With luck and endurance one could discover freedom; find a way to make God's law manifest in Man; or end up rich as a prince.

I) Irving Howe, American Newness

"Transport yourself to the past; imagine yourself in the America of one hundred and fifty years ago; suppose yourself alive at a moment when the new nation has started feeling its strength and boasting about its virtues—a moment also when the entire Western world is in ferment, with reform bills passed, slavery under attack, kings tottering, and new theories and inventions announced. This is the time in the United States of 'the newness,' when people start to feel socially invigorated and come to think they can act to determine their fate. What is it like to live at such a time? The opposite of what it is like to live today."

"Here in the young republic—'conceived in perfection,' Richard Hofstadter wittily says, 'and dedicated to progress'—a new mode of government has proved reasonably successful."

(5) RAW AND SAVAGE: ESTABLISHING DIFFERENCE FROM THE UNCIVILIZED AND THE IRRATIONAL

I) Joyce Warren, The American Narcissus

"Perhaps the best way to understand the consequences to other people of the American emphasis on individualism in the nineteenth century is to examine one of its most significant expressions at that time: the phenomenon of manifest destiny. The individual pioneer and frontiersman had been moving westward onto Indian land since the seventeenth century, and nineteenth-century Americans evolved a theory to justify this encroachment and such government acquisitions as Oregon, California, and Texas. The expanding American nation in the nineteenth century was an extension of the expanding individual—individualism writ large. What had begun as a movement of individuals became government policy. Most Americans would have agreed with journalist *Samuel Bowles, who, after a trip west, wrote in 1869: 'We should stop making treaties with tribes . . . we know they are not our equals; we know that our right to the soil, as a race capable of its superior improvement is above theirs.' The Indian, said Bowles, is 'the victim of our destiny . . . It is his destiny to die.'*

"A corollary of manifest destiny is, of course, the belief that the other guy, the victim of your destiny, does not count. This is the other side of American individualism, the side that is visible only if we look at individualism not from the point of view of the individual but from the point of view of the 'other'—the person or persons whom the individual sees as either useful to or standing in the way of his expansion."

II) ?

"Governor Peter Chester, newly arrived in the colony in 1770, understood the situation clearly. . . . They were not men of property, to be sure, Chester recognized, but neither were they the outlaws and thuggish riffraff that infested the back-country of all the colonies. They were industrious people who 'either could not subsist upon the barren lands on the back parts of the provinces from whence they came, or could not afford to pay to proprietors such sums as they demanded, and were therefore induced to emigrate into a country of whose fertility of soil and temperature of climate they had received such favourable accounts, in order to better their circumstances.' Such people could not contribute capital to the development of the province, but they 'can labour, and will make very good *first settlers. . . .* These sort of people however insignificant they may appear, are the only persons we can expect that will first attempt to settle an *uninhabited country, surrounded on all sides by numerous tribes of savages.*'"

III) ?

"To most Americans, the Indians were simply expendable nuisances, not people at all. This attitude is apparent in *Theodore Roosevelt's 1889 description of the settlement of the United States:* 'The white settler has merely moved into an *uninhabited* waste; he does not feel that he is committing a wrong, for he knows perfectly well that the land is really owned by no one. . . . The settler and pioneer have at bottom had justice on their side; this great continent could not have been kept as nothing but a game preserve for squalid savages.'"

One of the most interesting examples of the full play of an Africanistic Presence as savage, irrational, wild, insane in literature—for purposes of humor as well as narrative structure and progression—occurs in *Huckleberry Finn.*

"All of the terms of this description could be (and were) easily accommodated in Romanticism. Interestingly enough, American Romanticism seems to be the antithesis to the American Dream."

. . . its absence of hope, or realism, of materialism, or promise. For every burst of light, for every ray of optimism seems not only to be thrown into relief by its attendant shadow, but to be made up of this shadow. For a people who made much of their *"newness,"* their hope, their potential, their innocence, it is striking how dour, how troubled, how frightened, and how haunted the early founding literature is. There are words and labels for this haunting. Gothic, Romantic, Sermonic, for example, and there are precedents in the world from which they fled. The "affinity between the nineteenth-century American psyche and Gothic romance" is a clear one and much remarked upon.

"The great Romantics—such figures as William Wordsworth in England or Henry David Thoreau in the United States—*sought to turn from the artificial constraints of commercial civilization to what they saw as the superior truth of 'Nature.'*" *Col. History*, p. 426

"Emerson exhorted his contemporaries to reject fealty to the past: 'Let us demand our own works and laws and worship.'" [Hester Prynne: "Begin all anew! . . . The future is yet full of trial and success!"]

"Nevertheless, these ambitions [to make new] in the romances of the 1850s are always defeated by the force of circumstance and guilt and by the abiding pressure of the past." *Col. History,* p. 427 LH U.S.

The question I wish to put, however, is why a young country repelled by Europe's perceived horrors of corruption and swooning in a fit of desire and rejection devoted its talents to reproducing in its literature the typology of diabolism from which they and their fathers had fled. One could not benefit from the lessons of earlier mistakes and past misfortune without remembering them and protecting oneself from their repetition. Romance was the form in which a uniquely American drama could be played out. Not naturalism—that was much much later—not realism, hardly rationalism. Long after Europe had bid it goodbye, Romance remained the cherished expression of Young America. The question I wish to put is: What was there in American romanticism that made it so attractive a battle plain upon which to fight, to engage their demons? It does not seem to me to be the evasion of history that some have suggested it was. I find in it the head-on encounter with very real, very pressing historical forces and the contradictions inherent in those forces and which had been passed on to these writers. [*Consequences of individualism = loneliness of Escape to Nature = (Thoreau living near his mother). Problematic because chaotic. As well as Edenesque. Warren, p. 4, 12, 13, 16, 17*] *Romance, an exploration of anxiety imported from the shadows of European culture, made possible the sometimes safe and other times risky embrace of some very human, very American, very understandable fears. Their fear of being outcast, of failing, of powerlessness; their fear of boundarylessness, of Nature unbridled and with a capital N, of the absence of "civilization," of loneliness, of aggression both external and internal?* In short, their terrible fear of human freedom—the thing they coveted most of all? Romance offered writers not less, but more, not escape but entanglement. And for Young America it had everything. Nature symbolism, adventurous quests for the individual, opportunities for moralizing, fabulation, violence, incredibility, terror, and its most significant, overwhelming ingredient—darkness and all the connotative value it awakened. There is no romance free of what is called "the power of blackness," especially not in a country in which there was an incumbent population, already black, upon which the imagination could play; through whom historical, moral, metaphysical, and social fears, problems, and dichotomies could be articulated. Who, it could be assumed, offered themselves up as surrogate selves for meditation on these problems of human freedom—its lure and its elusiveness. Meditations on the terror of the outcast, the dread of failure, of powerlessness, of Nature without limits, of natal loneliness, of internal aggression, of evil, sin, greed as well as human potential and the rights of man.

Characteristics we looked at in the Dunbar cameo from Bailyn's book are not only intact themes in American literature, they are entrenched and expanded.

To enlightenment cum racism, authority, autonomy, newness, and the positing of a need for establishing a "civilizing" difference—we add two other allied characteristics that become themes: 1. is a haunting—a shadow haunts the works and their characters which is a problematization of past deprivations, and 2. claims and assertions of virility which are related to a desire for a future of power.

Melville offers us rich territory for tracing these themes, because instead of reducing them, he complicates them.

1. the partnership *enlightenment* and *racism*
   (Ch. 10, "Baron Friends")
2. authority
   (Ch. 1, white authority subverted/suicide/homicide p. 795
   Q (p. 847) serene self ease. White power ff. becomes the central idea of the text.)
3. autonomy
   mariners are individuals and free but ship is communal effort. Ahab's autonomy comes into question.
4. newness transformed into innocence and reverence for origineity & etymology
   I. as an innocent. P. also—but their innocence is not revered or privileged.
5. savage/civilized dichotomy of difference
   Spouter-wall, p. 806; Morning rites, p. 823
6. shadow as companion and surrogate
   Counterpane leading to *reverie,* p. 820
7. claims of virility and absolute power Sermon
   a) welcomes Jonah repentance b) tell the truth *via God's Word*
   Ahab
   Whale

Ernest Hemingway/Willa Cather

Each of the following lectures will focus on one of the five approaches listed on your syllabus, the five "routes of access" into Africanist literary discourse. Surrogate self as enabler; Africanist character; Africanist idiom; Africanist narrative; and becoming Other.

The "Surrogate Self as Enabler" simply means the use of blacks to aggrandize or explore the self. It is divided here into two parts (lectures). One (this one) is the codes and representations of Africanism in Hemingway and in Willa Cather.

The second lecture on surrogacy (October 8) is concerned with how hierarchical difference (not just difference but *ranked* difference) is constructed and more of the problems such construction causes within the work—as well as how singular and subtle and highly creative language and technique become in certain works when reinforcing white hegemony is not the work's explicit intention. *Moby-Dick* being a case in point.

But while blacks did not threaten Melville's white males so deeply that his crewmen and officers on the *Pequod* required isolation from them, or could not engage them on an equal and/or equalizing status, women may have been far more difficult for Melville to deal with.

Joyce Warren's *American Narcissus* contains an interesting analysis of his treatment of women—along with other nineteenth-century writers—if you are interested. The shore is well figured in most of his work as feminine; the sea, of course, is figured as masculine—although it can have feminine pronouns. But in *Pierre* and other of Melville's novels, there is ample opportunity for the development of female characters, as there is not in *Moby-Dick,* and it is fascinating to see how he handles those opportunities.

The placement and sequence of the fiction chosen to explicate these matters have additional significance. The construction of a white male that we have been tracing has serious implications for gender as well as race. White women are absorbed into this construction—sometimes acceding to it happily for the rewards it can deliver in power and status; other times suffering within that construction; being conflicted by it; and sometimes vigorously resisting it. The three novels to be discussed this week reveal what the implications of Africanism are for women characters. The enabling role of Africanism for men becomes disabling for women. What supports white male hegemony does not seem to offer similar support to white women without a debt difficult to defer.

The fissures in the combination of white male power and white female relationship to that power are dramatically exposed by the presence of Africanist personae in the work. The sexual equation of white male and female *required* a sexualized black presence. It is as though without it, there could be no negotiation of, nor sharing of, nor acquiescence to white male power.

You will understand how severe the sexual constraints had to be. Think of it: if white women had refused the privilege and status on the terms men offered in the 19th century, they, the women, could have wiped out the entire white male population in one generation and replaced it with a black (or "mixed," as they say) population.

To track these changes, assumptions, and appropriations, I begin with the novel reported to be deliberately "political." In *To Have and Have Not,* Harry Morgan, the central figure in this work, seems to represent (or replicate) the classic American hero: a solitary man battling a government that would limit his freedom and his individuality; he is romantically and sentimentally respectful of the Nature he destroys for a living (deep-sea fishing); competent, street-wise, "knowing" and impatient with those who are not; virile, risk-taking and risk-loving, and so right and guiltless in his account of himself to himself it seems a shame to question his reflections or challenge them. Before we do challenge them, we should examine how Hemingway shows the reader that Harry is knowing, virile, free, brave, and moral.

In chapter one, on page ten, Harry includes a nigger in his crew, a nigger who at this point in Harry's first-person voice has no name. His appearance is signaled by the sentence "Just then this nigger we had getting bait comes down the dock." The black man is not only nameless for the whole of the chapter, he is somehow not even hired. He is someone "we had getting bait." A kind of trained response, not a job. His selection, objected to by the white client, Johnson, is defended by Harry on the basis of the black man's skill. He "put on a nice bait and he was fast." The rest of the time, we are told, this nameless black sleeps and reads the papers.

Something very curious happens to this namelessness when the author shifts voices. Whenever Harry thinks about this black man in chapter one, he thinks "nigger." Later, when Hemingway uses the third-person point of view, narrating and representing Harry's speech, two formulations of this black man occur: he both remains nameless and stereotyped and becomes named, and personalized. Harry says "Wesley" when speaking to the black man in direct dialogue; Hemingway *writes* "nigger" when referring to him. Needless to report, this black man is never identified as one. Part Two, written in the third person, reserves and repeats this phrase, "The man," for Harry. The spatial and conceptual difference is marked by the shortcut that the term "nigger" allows with all of its color/caste implications; and the term occupies a territory between man and animal and thus withholds specificity while marking it. Also, needless to report, this black character either does not speak (as a nigger) or speaks in very legislated and manipulated ways (as a Wesley). Enforcing silence proves troubling to the author and requires of him some extraordinary measures. At a crucial moment [p. 13] during the fishing expedition, which has disappointed both the captain and his customer because they've found no catch, the boat enters into promising waters. Harry is coaching Johnson; the black man is at the wheel, although we have been assured that he does nothing aside from cutting bait but read and sleep. Harry can't do it all, it appears—be in two critical places at the same time: instructing the incompetent Johnson and guiding the vessel—at least not in a narrative that accepts these logical limits. But there is another person aboard: an alcoholic named Eddy, too unreliable to be given this responsibility, although he is given manhood and speech and a physical description. Eddy is white and we know he is because he is not identified as such. Now, with Harry taking care of his customer, Eddy in a pleasant stupor—there is only the nigger man to tend the wheel. When the sign heralding the promising waters arrives—the sighting of flying fish beyond the prow of the boat—the crewman facing the phenomenon ought to be the first to see them. In fact he is the first to see them. The problem is how to acknowledge that first sighting and continue the muzzling of this "nigger" who, so far, has not said one word. The solution to this problem is a strangely awkward, oddly constructed sentence: "The nigger was still taking her out and I looked and saw he had seen a patch of flying fish burst out ahead. . . ." "Saw he had seen" is an improbable construction in syntax, sense, and tense, but like other choices available to Hemingway it is risked to avoid a speaking black. The problem this writer gives himself, therefore, is saying how one sees that someone else has already seen. A better, certainly more graceful, choice would be to have the black man cry out at the sighting, but the logic of the discrimination prevents a verbal initiative that has importance to the business Harry is involved in to come from this so far nameless, sexless, nationless

Africanistic presence. It is the powerful one, the authoritative one, who sees. The power of looking is Harry's; the passive powerlessness is the black man's, but he, the black man, does not speak of it. Silencing him, refusing him the opportunity of one important word forces the author to abandon his search for clarity and to set up a curiously silent mate/captain relationship. What would have been the cost, I wonder, of humanizing, genderizing, this character at the opening of the novel? For one thing, Harry would have to be compared to a helpless alcoholic and a contemptible customer—neither of whom carries the sexual excitement, the possible threat to virility and competence, the suggestion of violence under wraps, and neither of whom can be assumed to be in some way bound, fixed, unfree, and serviceable. The proximity and intimacy to violence is stressed at once in the novel, before the black crewman's entrance, by the slaughter in the bar during which the Cubans are singled out as black and not black, and in which the blacks are the most gratuitously violent and savage. "The nigger with the Tommy gun got his face almost into the street and gave the back of the wagon a burst from underneath and sure enough one came down, . . . at ten feet the nigger shot him in the belly with the Tommy gun, with what must have been the last shot . . . old Pancho sat down hard and went over forwards. He was trying to come up, still holding onto the Luger, only he couldn't get his head up, when the nigger took the shotgun that was lying against the wheel of the car by the chauffeur and blew the side of his head off. Some nigger." [p. 8]

In Part Two, where Harry and the black crewman do engage in dialogue, and the black talks a great deal, the serviceability of the black is completely without subtlety. What he says and when he says [it] is plotted to win admiration for Harry. First of all, Wesley's speech falls into two categories: 1. grumbles and complaints, and 2. apologies for weakness. Secondly, we hear the grumbles, the groans, the weakness as Wesley's responses to his gunshot wounds for three pages before we learn that Harry is also shot, and much worse than Wesley is. In fact, Harry has not only not mentioned his own pain, he has nursed and comforted Wesley, taken his abuse, done the difficult work of steering and tossing the contraband overboard in elegant, stoic gestures of manliness. Deferring information about Harry's more serious pain while we listen to Wesley: "I'm shot . . ." "You're just scared." "No, sir. I'm shot. And I'm hurting bad. I've been throbbing all night." . . . "I hurt . . . I hurt worse all the time." "I'm sorry, Wesley," the man said. "But I got to steer." "You treat a man no better than a dog," the nigger said. He was getting ugly now. But the man was still sorry for him. [p. 69] Finally, this exchange: "Who the hell's shot worse?" he asked him. "You or me?" "You're shot worse," the nigger said . . . [p. 70]

The use and positioning of "nigger," "Wesley," and a solitary "Negro" may seem arbitrary and confusing, but in fact it is carefully structured. Harry, in dialogue with a helpmate, cannot say "nigger" without offending the reader (if not the helpmate)—so he uses his name. No such responsibility is taken on, however, by the legislating narrator who always uses the generative and degrading term. "The nigger blubbered with his face against a sack. The man went on slowly lifting the sacked packages of liquor and dropping them over the side." (Nigger said—man said) [p. 75] But once Wesley has apologized, recognized and accepted his inferiority, Harry can and does use "nigger," along with the proper name, in direct dialogue—in familiar camaraderie: "Mr. Harry," said the nigger, "I'm sorry I couldn't help dump that stuff." "Hell," said Harry, "ain't no nigger any good when he's shot. You're a all right nigger, Wesley." [p. 87]

I mentioned two main categories of speech for the black man: grumbles and apology. But there is a third. Throughout the exchange, while the two men are suffering—one stoically, one whimperingly—the black man criticizes the white man in lapses of whimperings and terror. They are interesting lapses because they describe an antagonist Harry, and because such lapses occur over and over again in Hemingway's fiction. Accusations of inhumanity, and, in other words, prophecies of doom in the mouths of the blacks that people his work. "Ain't a man's life worth more than a load of liquor?" Wesley asks Harry. "Why don't people be honest and decent and make a decent honest living? You don't care what happens to a man . . . You ain't hardly human." "You ain't human," the nigger said. "You ain't got human feelings." In other works threats and promises of madness, intuitions of death [*tk*] are put into the mouths of black characters.

The serviceability I have been describing becomes even more pronounced and exploited when Hemingway begins to describe male and female relationships. In this same novel, the last voice we hear is that of Harry's devoted wife, Marie, crediting and celebrating the virtues, the goodness, the virility, the bravery of her husband who is now dead. [*READ pp. 258–*] She recalls him fondly as "snotty and strong and quick, and like some kind of expensive animal. It would always get me to just watch him move." Immediately following this encomium of sexuality and power and revered (expensive) brutality, she meditates on her hatred of Cubans (the Cubans killed Harry) and says they are "bad luck for Conchs . . ." and ". . . bad luck for anybody. They got too many niggers there too." This judgment is followed by her recollection of a trip she and Harry took to Havana when she was 26 years old. Harry had a lot of money then and while they walked in the park a nigger (as opposed to a Cuban—although the black man she is referring to is both black and Cuban) "said something" to Marie and Harry smacked him and threw his straw hat into the street where a taxi ran over it. Marie remembers laughing "so hard it made her belly ache." With nothing but a paragraph indentation between them, the next reverie is a further association of Harry with sexuality, power, and protection. It was the first time she "made her hair blonde." The two anecdotal recollections are connected in time and place and, significantly, connected by color coding as sexual coding. We do not know what the black man said, but the horror is that he said anything at all. It is enough that he spoke, claimed an intimacy perhaps, but certainly claimed a view, and inserted his sexual self into their space and their consciousness as a speaking, therefore, aggressive presence, since he initiated the remark. In the telling, with warm remembrance, several stereotypical elements are present: sexuality, violence, class, and the retribution of an impartial machine. The couple, Marie and Harry, is young and in love with obviously enough money to feel and be powerful in Cuba. Into that Eden comes the violating nigger making impertinent remarks. The disrespect, which probably had sexual overtones, is punished at once by Harry's violence—he smacks the black man, and further picks up his straw hat (the straw identifies the class, I should think), destroying the black man's property, just as the black man had sullied Harry's property (his wife). When the taxi, inhuman, onrushing, impartial machine, runs over the hat, it is as though the universe had acquiesced in Harry's justifiable response. It is that underscoring that makes Marie laugh. That and her obvious comfort in and adulation of this "strong and quick" husband of hers. What follows in the beauty parlor is positioned as interdependent on the episode of black invasion of privacy and intimation of sexuality from which Marie must be protected. The urgency to establish difference—a difference within the sexual context—is commanding. Marie tells us how she is transformed from black to white, from dark to blonde. A painful and difficult process that turns out to be well worth the pain in its sexual, protective, differentiating payout. "They were working on it all afternoon and it was naturally so dark they didn't want to do it . . . but I kept telling them to see if they couldn't make it a little lighter . . . and all I'd say was just see if you can't make it a little lighter." When the bleaching and perming is done, Marie's satisfaction is decidedly sensual, if not explicitly sexual. "When I put my hand and touched it, and I couldn't believe it was me and I was so excited I was choked with it . . . I was so excited feeling all funny inside, sort of faint like . . ." It's a genuine transformation. Marie becomes a self she can hardly believe, she is so golden and soft and silky. Her own sensual reaction to her whitening is echoed by Harry, who sees her and says, "Jesus, Marie, you're beautiful." And when she wants to hear more about her beauty, he tells her not to talk—just "Let's go to the hotel." This enhanced sexuality comes on the heels of a sexual intrusion by a black man. What would have been the consequence if the insult to Marie had come from a white man? Would the bleaching have followed? And if so, would it have been in such lush and sexually heightened language? What does establishing a difference from darkness to lightness accomplish for the concept of oneself as sexually alive and potent? So powerful, so coherent in the world? These tourists in Havana meet an inhabitant of that city and have a privileged status in it because they are white. But to assure us that this status is deserved, they encounter a molesting, physically inferior black male representative of illicit sexuality which spurs the narrative to a higher, better, sexier, legal, white counterpart.

The metonymic fetishizing of color, transferring to blackness the power of illicit sexuality, chaos, madness, impropriety, becomes standard treatment of Africanism in the posthumously published novel, *The Garden of Eden.*

Willa Cather offers us a chance to examine an extraordinary novel: *Sapphira and the Slave Girl.* References to this novel in Cather scholarship have been apologetic, dismissive, or cutting in their brief documentation of its flaws—of which there are a sufficient number. What remains less acknowledged is the source of its flaws and the extraordinary nature of the conceptual problems the book both poses and represents. It is as though this last book—this troublesome, quietly dismissed novel, so important to Cather—is itself a fugitive from her literary estate—which may be because it *concerns* a fugitive—a fugitive slave girl—and *describes/*inscribes the narrative's own fugitive flight from itself.

Our first hint of this flight resides in the title, *Sapphira and the Slave Girl.* The girl referred to is named Nancy. To have titled the book "Sapphira and Nancy" would have lured Miss Cather into dangerously deep water. Such a title would have clarified and drawn attention immediately to what the novel obscures even while it makes a valiant effort at honest engagement: the sycophancy of white identity.

The story, briefly, is this.

Sapphira Colbert, an invalided slave mistress, confined to her chair and dependent on slaves for the most intimate services, has persuaded herself that her husband is having or aching to have a liaison with Nancy, the pubescent daughter of Mistress Colbert's most devoted female slave. It is clear from the beginning that Miss Colbert is in error: Nancy is pure to the point of vapidity; Master Colbert is a man of modest habits, ambition, and imagination.

Sapphira's suspicions, fed by her feverish imagination and by her license to have them, grow and luxuriate unbearably. She forms a plan. She will invite a malleable lecherous nephew, Martin, to visit and let his nature run its course. Nancy will be seduced, but in fact not "ruined" and, though it is not mentioned, it is clearly understood that this may even produce another body for Miss Colbert to own. The purpose of arranging the rape of her young servant is to reclaim, for purposes not made clear, the full attention of her husband.

Interfering with these plans is Sapphira's daughter, Rachel, estranged from her mother for her abolitionist views primarily, but also, we are led to believe, because Sapphira does not tolerate opposition. It is Rachel who manages to effect Nancy's escape to the North and freedom with the timid help of her father, Master Colbert. A reconciliation of all of the white parties takes place when the daughter loses one of her children to diphtheria and is blessed with the recuperation of the other. The reconciliation of the two key black characters is rendered in a postscript in which many years later Nancy returns to see her aged mother and recount her post-flight adult narrative to the author, a child witnessing the return and the happiness that is the novel's denouement. The novel was published in 1940, but has the shape and feel of a tale written or experienced much earlier.

Our interest in this novel is related to both its complexities and its problems. Both arise, I believe, not because Miss Cather was failing in narrative power, but because of her struggle to address an almost completely buried subject: the interdependent working of power, race, and sexuality in a white woman's battle for coherence.

In some ways this novel is a classic fugitive slave narrative: the thrilling escape of the bound into freedom. Except that we learn practically nothing of the trials of the fugitive's journey because the emphasis is on Nancy's fugitive state *within* the household *before her escape.* Except that the real fugitive, the text asserts, is the slave mistress. Except that the plot itself is a fugitive from the author.

Let me take these points in order. Escape is the central focus of Nancy's existence on the Colbert farm. From the moment of her first appearance, she is forced to hide—her emotions, her thoughts, and eventually her body from pursuers. Unable to please Sapphira, plagued by the jealousy of other darker slaves, she is also barred from help, instruction, or consolation from her own mother, Till. This latter condition could only prevail in a slave society in which the mistress can count on (or an author can perceive that the mistress can count on) and the reader does not object to the complicity of a mother in the seduction/rape of her own daughter. A mother whose loyalty to and responsibility for her mistress is so primary, it never occurs and need not occur to Sapphira that Till might be hurt, or alarmed by the violence planned for her only child. That assumption is based on another—that slave women are not mothers; that they are "natally dead," having no obligations and seeking none regarding their offspring or their ancestors.

This breach startles the contemporary reader and renders Till an unbelievable and unsympathetic character. It is a problem that Cather seems herself hard put to address, and is forced, I reckon, to come to terms with this wholly unanalyzed mother/daughter relationship by inserting a furtive exchange between Till and Rachel that seems to come out of nowhere because there has been nothing in a hundred or so pages to prepare us for that maternal concern. "You ain't heard nothin?" Till asks of Rachel. Is Nancy all right? Did she arrive safely? Is she alive? Is anybody after her? All of those questions lie in the one she does manage to ask.

Surrounding that question is the silence of four hundred years. It leaps out of the novel's void and out of the void of historical discourse on the slave parent/children relationships and pain. The contemporary reader is relieved when Till finally finds language and occasion to make this inquiry about the life or death of her daughter. But since nothing more is made of it, it seems clear that Cather was driven to create the exchange not to rehabilitate Till in our readerly eyes but because at some point the silence became an unbearable kind of violence within a text loaded with violence and evasion. The need to have and portray the faithful slave; the compelling attraction of exploring the fictional possibilities of one woman's absolute power over the body of another woman; the need to make credible the unearned bottomless devotion of the body upon which Sapphira is totally dependent. It is, after all, *hers,* this slave woman's body, in a way that her own invalid flesh is not. These fictional demands stretch to breaking all narrative coherence. It is no wonder that Nancy is helpless to think up her own escape and must be urged into taking its risk.

Nancy must therefore hide her interior life from hostile co-slaves, *and* her own mother. The absence of camaraderie between Nancy and the other slave women turns on the device of the color fetish—the skin color privilege Nancy enjoys because she is lighter than the others, and therefore enviable. The absence of mother love turns on natal isolation that Cather herself had trouble representing. These are bizarre and disturbing assumptions that normally lie mute in novels containing Africanist characters, but which Cather is unwilling to repress altogether. Thus her character is at once a fugitive within the household and a sign of the defenselessness of character credibility when there is no available language to clarify or even name the source of unbelievability.

Interestingly, the other major cause of Nancy's constant state of flight is wholly credible. That she should be unarmed in the face of the sexual assault of the nephew, and that she is alone responsible for extracting herself from this crisis is wholly credible. We do not question the vulnerability of a young girl being pursued by a cad. What becomes titillating in this wickedness pursuing innocence—what makes it something other than an American variant of *Clarissa*—is the racial component. The nephew is not even required to court or seduce Nancy. He can, and plans to, simply arrive where she is sleeping. And since Sapphira has ordered her to sleep in the hall on a pallet, Nancy is forced to sneak away in the dark to quarters where she may be, but is not certain to be, safe. Other than Rachel, the pro-abolitionist, Nancy has access to no one to whom she can complain, explain, object or from whom she can seek protection. We must accept her lack of initiative of any kind, for there are no exits. She has no recourse—except her miserable looks that arouse Rachel's curiosity.

There is no law, if the nephew Martin succeeds in the rape, that would even entertain her complaint. If she becomes pregnant and delivers a child as a result of the proposed violence, the issue is a boon to the economy of the farm and the mill, not an injury to it. There is no father, or, in this case, "stepfather" to voice a protest on her behalf since honor was the first thing stripped from him. He is a "capon," we are told, given to Till so she will have no more children and can give her full attention and energy to Mistress Sapphira.

Rendered voiceless, a cipher, a perfect victim, Nancy runs the risk of losing the reader's interest in her, although not in her plight. For, in a curious way, Sapphira's plotting, like Cather's plot, is without reference to the characters and is solely for the benefit of ego-gratification. This becomes obvious when we consider what would have been the consequences of a successful rape. Given the novel's own terms, there can be no grounds for Sapphira thinking Nancy can be "ruined" in the conventional sense. There is no question of marriage to Martin, to Colbert, to anybody. Why would such an assault put her slave girl outside her husband's interest rather than secure it? If Master Colbert is tempted by Nancy the chaste, is there anything in slavocracy to make him disdain Nancy the unchaste?

Such a breakdown in the logic of plot construction is rampant with implications for the impact of race on narrative—and on narrative strategy. Nancy becomes the victim not only of Sapphira's evil, whimsical scheming. She becomes the unconsulted, appropriated ground of Cather's inquiry into what is of paramount importance to the author: the reckless, unabated power of a white woman gathering identity unto herself from the wholly available and serviceable lives of Africanist Others. These recognitions seem to be to provide the coordinates of an immensely important moral debate.

This novel is not a story of a mean, vindictive mistress. It is the story of a desperate one. It concerns a barren, disappointed woman confined to the prison of her defeated flesh, whose social pedestal rests on the sturdy spine of racial degradation; whose privileged gender has nothing that elevates it except color, and whose moral posture collapses without a whimper before the greater necessity of self-esteem regardless of the fact that it is a delusion. For Sapphira too is a fugitive in this novel, a fugitive committed to escape: from the possibility of developing her own adult personality, her own sensibilities; from her femaleness; from motherhood; from the community of women; from her body.

She escapes the necessity of inhabiting her own body by dwelling on the young and healthy and sexually appetizing Nancy. She has transferred its care into the hands of others. In this way she escapes her illness, her decay, her confinement, her anonymity, and her physical powerlessness. In other words, she has the leisure and the instruments to construct a self; but the self she constructs must be—is conceivable only as—"white." The surrogate black bodies become her hands, her feet, her fantasies of sexual ravish, a surrogate intimacy with her husband, and, not inconsiderably, her sole source of love.

If the Africanist characters and their condition are removed from the text of *Sapphira and the Slave Girl* we will not have Miss Haversham immured or in flames. We have nothing: no process of deranged self-construction that can take for granted acquiescence in so awful an enterprise; no drama of limitless power. Sapphira can hide far more successfully than Nancy. She can remain, and does remain outside the normal requirements of adult womanhood because of the infantilized Africanist population at her disposal.

The final fugitive in Cather's novel is the novel itself. The plot's own plotting to free the endangered slave girl (of no apparent interest, as we have noted, to the girl's mother or her slave associates) is designed for quite other purposes. It functions as a means for the author to meditate on the moral equivalence of free white women with enslaved black ones. The fact that these equations are designed as mother-daughter pairings and relationships makes the conclusion that Cather was dreaming and re-dreaming her problematic relationship with her own mother inescapable.

The imaginative strategy is a difficult one at best, an impossible one in the event. So impossible that Cather permits the novel to leave, to escape from the pages of fiction into nonfiction and non sequitur. For narrative credibility she substitutes her own determination to force the equation. It is an equation that must take place outside the narrative. The text of *Sapphira and the Slave Girl* turns at the end into a kind of memoir, the author's recollection of herself as a child witnessing the return and reconciliation and an imposed "all rightness" in untenable, outrageous circumstance. The silenced, acquiescent Africanist characters in the narrative are not less muzzled in the epilogue. The reunion—the drama of it, like its narrative function—is no more the slave characters' than their slave lives have been. The reunion is literally stage-managed for the author become child. Till agrees to wait until little Willa is there at the doorway before she permits herself the very first sight she has had of her daughter in twenty-five years.

Only with Africanist characters is such a project of delayed gratification for the pleasure of a (white) child thinkable. When the embrace is over, Willa the white child accompanies the black mother and daughter into their narrative, listening to the dialogue but intervening in it at every turn. The shape and detail and substance of their lives are hers—not theirs. Just as Sapphira employed these surrogate, serviceable black bodies for her own purposes of power without risk, so the author employs them on behalf of her own desire for a safe participation in loss, in love, in chaos, in justice.

But things go awry. As often happens, characters make claims, impose demands of imaginative accountability over and above the author's will to contain them. Just as Rachel's intervention foils Sapphira's plot, so Cather's urgent need to know and understand this Africanist mother and daughter requires her to give them center stage. The child Cather listens to Till's stories, and the slave, silenced in the narrative, has the final words of the epilogue.

In returning to her childhood, at the end of her writing career, Cather returns to a very personal, indeed private experience. In her last novel she works out and toward the meaning of female betrayal as it faces the void of racialism. She may not have arrived safely, like Nancy, but she did undertake the dangerous journey.

Flannery O'Connor/
Carson McCullers

The novels of Ernest Hemingway, as well as most fiction of the twenties, thirties, and forties, are no longer obliged to do the technically strenuous work of establishing racial difference that we observed in the nineteenth century with Edgar Allan Poe. The negative "other," the freely available surrogate, is already convention so entrenched, it seems "natural." The writer has only to observe the rules, employ any combination of the codes that move about in social/cultural discourse: make sure the Africanist character is never without the sign of color or other marks of racial identification; never identify him or her as a citizen of a country or state; never give black personae power other than the power to serve; nor any voice other than comic, cowardly, obsequious, unreasonable, illicit, or de-sexed—*unless* the voice reinforces the status quo. Since the codes are already embedded, what startles us now are the ways in which writers illuminate and reveal them, dismiss them or disentangle them. It is still possible to write Negro or nigger and rely comfortably on the reader's comprehension of what all of that signifies; but it also becomes possible to load the term with irony. It is still possible to write *Sapphira and the Slave Girl* to ensure more or less complete communication because if the title were *Sapphira and Nancy* the power relationship would be out of kilter, off balance, because what would we feel if Sapphira called in her nephew to sexually assault a girl or woman who is not a slave? How could the reader be so sure that there would be no legal recourse Nancy could take, no risk to Sapphira? No demur or hesitation from the nephew. How could we believe that not only is escape illegal, so is remedy. And how could a reader accept the possibility that there would be no objection from Nancy's mother? Such is the nature of slavery and the assumptions folded into that system. But such things do occur to Willa Cather, and when they do they surprise us, and relieve us. We are relieved that Nancy's welfare does matter to [Cather and] Till—that social death and natal isolation (in this case) is not complete. For if it is, then Till is thoroughly demonized, robotized either by slavery or something "innate" in her different genes. Although Cather's novel was published in 1940, we seem not to need the historical frame of slavery for the story to exude credibility. Faulkner's Africanist characters situated in mid-twentieth century could very easily respond the same way as Blue Bell, Jeff. [The difference between Nancy's flight for her life, and the flight of the young black man in the film *Crimes of the Heart* is the mode of transportation.] And the possibility of a virile and serious and seriously taken black man—all three—is ignored in virtually the entire world of Cather's and Hemingway's fiction.

Still, the most glaring assumptions of these novels, so far—Melville's work being an exception—is the social death of the Africanist characters—they either have no family context or obligations, or if they do have family, they are irrelevant emotionally to the black person and certainly to the whites. Their condition is timeless, history-less, without a cultural context other than their convenience or inconvenience to white culture. In short, they are bodies—for labor or exploitation; or they are shadows that haunt, hound, or threaten; or they are shadows that protect and guide. Willa Cather in the very act of confronting these anomalies has recourse to distancing language, linguistic shortcuts, and although she does more than many to avail herself of a writer's obligation to chart or imply a character's interior life from some reliable point of view, Miss Cather rests too much of her case in character description on such hopelessly inadequate characteristics as skin color: the very black being evil, the lighter skinned being good. And carnal knowledge: what, for example, does Jeff think about his position, his castration, his wife, his stepdaughter?

By the time we get to Flannery O'Connor, we can see just as clearly as the old grandfather does the "artificial nigger" on the lawn and it is to O'Connor's credit and her astonishing powers of observation that she knew all about it and put it on display. Showing us exactly what estranging devices are inherent in Africanism, and what purposes they serve in a white male consciousness and ultimately in literature itself.

Had I not had to submit a course title respectable enough to pass muster with the Committee on Academic Instruction, I would have called this course, or subtitled it, the same title Flannery O'Connor gave to the story by her I've asked you to read.

Apparently Miss O'Connor believed it her most satisfactory story. It isn't mine—there are several of hers I find most and more satisfactory—but for the purposes of this discussion, it is as perfect and as perfectly written as a short piece of fiction can be—both identifying the thesis of this course and dramatizing that thesis.

For O'Connor the questions are these: How does Mr. Head come to deserve *mercy,* God's forgiveness, self-realization, reconciliation through and because of this child abuse and treachery? Is the treachery the education he wished to and succeeded in giving him, or his cowardice in denying his grandson? The latter, of course, is what the character is concerned with, that he has mercifully recognized *Original Sin* and been spared, seen his sinful nature and been permitted to repent of it. The sin, however, is both the denial of the grandson and the denial *to* the grandson of the grandson's own *body* (i.e., having shown him the bodily distance from and alienness of black bodies, he strips the boy of a connection with his own body: the desire, hunger, and longing he felt in the presence of the black woman. Now that feeling of hunger is shame. Is O'Connor in collusion with Mr. Head? Has she also employed the *artificial nigger* as the unifying force, the thing about which one must know like the serpent which is the train leaving the safe haven, the home, the Eden they left for the educational journey to the city? How has the religious trope subverted and blinded the characters and possibly O'Connor herself? Her letters might provide some clarity here, but one should be warned about equating racial tolerance or racial hatred with the exigencies of a written text. Is this a story about a touch of and by evil, and how is it given to us to recognize it (evil) out there and in us, and that with the grace of God we can attain salvation? If so, the geography of the nigger has several roles to play, some known and understood on the surface, some subcutaneous, and some perhaps subliminal: Afro-Americans as "lost territory," "wilderness" [the experience in the neighborhood]; as a "fall" into desire, vulnerability to which is weakness and the absence of "sense" ["You act like you don't have any sense!" p. 262] and brute, animal ignorance ["standing there grinning like a chim-pan-zee while a nigger woman gives you direction. Great Gawd!" p. 263]. After which is closure—the lesson is learned: to listen to a nigger, especially a nigger *woman,* is to be like an unreasoning animal, not human, alien to the species; Afro-Americans as both that from which humans (whites) *do* flee and that from which humans *must* flee, if they are to be known as and to understand themselves as *human* and to have a *place* among humankind. In other words, the question of who am I is answered with *I am not them.* Not "Je pense, therefore j'existe," but the definition of self by what one is disconnected from. Affirmation by negation. And into this dilemma, this problem of identification, steps the ever merciful hand of O'Connor's God saying, in effect: "Now you know evil, have been tempted by it, surrendered to it, suffered from its presence, and I offer you grace and salvation as a result of your acknowledgment that to stray into the wilderness is forbidden by Me." Substituting niggers for the pronouns and nouns, God's admonition reads as follows: "Now you have seen, encountered known *niggers,* have been tempted into identifying with *niggers,* have surrendered to *niggers,* have suffered the consequence of the presence of *niggers* and have received My grace, mercy, and forgiveness because you admit that the wilderness of *niggers* is forbidden to you."

It is clear, therefore, that regardless of the apparently empathetic, sympathetic, even distantly objective stated view of Blacks, the text speaks another tale, one consistent with the habit of American fiction to engage Afro-Americans only as inventions of and the demands of the imagination to construct a self [in this sense the *nigger* is "artificial," meaning *made* up], and to reconcile the contradictions inherent in this construct by a retreat into (in this case) the claims of a moral universe. To, in fact, *summon* black presences in order to define what it is to *be.* The silence of the heretic is instructive here, that is, the blacks speak only to (1) not be heard (softly, in the train), (2) make haughty claims but not about themselves (the waiter's instructions), their claims are haughty because they reproduce the white man's rules, and (3) lastly (the woman in Atlanta) to help. The black people who do not serve the master narrative cannot be heard, because it is possible that the voices too soft to be heard may be engaged in conversation about themselves—a conversation to which O'Connor is not privy, and even if she were to invent, imagine it, such a conversation would destabilize the story. Derail it. Lose, as Mr. Head does, the *tracks* altogether. Note that Mr. Head cannot understand or bring himself to understand the black woman's perfectly accurate advice about how to find his way back; but the white man with the dogs *is* understandable, and what is more, lives in a neighborhood adjacent to the railroad stop that is their only hope of getting home at all—three blocks away, and they arrive just in the nick of time. In this sense, the good middle class white man (with dogs) is the saving deus ex machina. And the "artificial" nigger proves to be not just made, not just made up, but *summoned* by the author for a safe engagement with mortal sin.

One of the questions to be explored in the assigned fiction is how does the work perceive and then employ the benefits of "knowing" an Africanist persona; what are the consequences of that knowledge to the knower? Once the work establishes whether and how it knows, what satisfaction or dissatisfaction follows? Is the knower more in control? Does he or she behave differently and in what way?

At the opening of "The Artificial Nigger" the reader is lured into a vision of what there is to yearn for and to protect. And once the seduction is complete we are quickly deprived of the vision of power, elegance, and class superiority. [p. 249—"Mr. Head had awakened . . ."]

Mr. Head's dreams of power are dashed by O'Connor with "overturned bucket beside the chair." But before that we learn that he has one major source of strength left: the ability to be "a suitable guide to the young." Although this "young" is a dark spot.

The balance of the story is the rite of passage, the education, the distribution of "knowledge" to a white male child. To change him from a dark spot to a white one. [p. 241] But this sojourn, likened to Virgil's, is education by deprivation—a kind of child abuse in its point and in its strategies. The goal—to know a "nigger"—is at once put forth as almost the sole objective of the "teaching" Mr. Head has to offer his grandson. [top p. 252] This, it turns out, is the documentation of such knowledge there is for the rite of passage to adulthood. Mr. Head is "showing Nelson that 'he ain't as smart as he thinks he is.'" He is initiating him into the limits of life and the pangs of "reality." He believes this to be his duty as a good grandfather: to warn, to name, to demonstrate, etc. A paradigm of the ancient initiation in forest or jungle. Africanist people, therefore, become the thing and its symbol: the battle plain upon which this initiation takes place. Once we learn that the area to be known is some body of knowledge known as "nigger," the second step is of contact—of actually sighting and identifying the area here represented as the physical Africanist body as well as the body of knowledge. And the knowledge to be gained is that it is different and that the difference is lesser in all of its details. [p. 252: "You ain't never seen . . ."] It is also important that in the process of identification, the warning, and the context in which this knowledge of difference should be held.{??} Third is to show the novice how to behave with, toward, or in the company of the Africanist presence in order to gather unto oneself courage, dominance, and power. This last is actually unavailable to Mr. Head, so he settles for contempt, and wit to cover ignorance as in the dining car scene. And, when in Atlanta, and the two of them are lost in a colored neighborhood—it is the ultimate nightmare of the forest: to be lost among them without protection or resources of defense. It is the boy, Nelson, who ventures to ask directions and to feel desire for the black woman who gives him information about how to get out of the forest. The consequence of this teaching and knowing offered by the grandfather is recommended form of behavior linked to and cultivated as part of what in the world there is to know to support, perhaps, the visions of beauty and power and class superiority the story opens with. It does not matter what the black people are really like—now that the knowledge has been transferred, the knower need only find support for the veracity of the knowledge, even if he discovers exceptions to it. How Nelson is reformulated from one who feels desire to one who feels detestation (as well as shame for having desired) is the remarkable achievement of both the story and the storyteller and the system that requires it.

It is significant that the first step in knowing this Africanist topography is limited to the sighting of the skin, the color of the skin. Nelson complains, "But you said niggers were black not tan." It's hard not to put the question of whether Flannery O'Connor was being impartial and realistically objective in her descriptions of the blacks. Her descriptive terms of Mr. Head and Nelson are ghostly pale; she stresses their aversion to looking at themselves; they have a self-loathing which is consistently implied when they catch sight of themselves. Contrast this self-loathing with the absence of it in the descriptions for the black characters. [p. 254 . . . "A huge coffee-colored man . . ."]

This man, followed by two young colored women who are talking softly, walking purposefully, the ruby, the sapphire, the walking stick, the gaze—may suggest excess to us, but would be an envied opulence to both Mr. Head and Nelson. Then there is the expert powerful-in-this-context demeanor of the waiters. [pp. 256–57] And in Atlanta the watching, unself-conscious children, the black woman to whom Nelson is attracted with a passion that is as seductive as it is maternal. This woman's hair is a mess, but she fondles it; her body is described as unattractive, but desirable. She gives helpful information and caressing speech: "sugarpie." [p. 261] There is a conflict between the description of their bodies and their absence of self-loathing. What then is there to say, in this story, about love and the body, knowledge as weaponry and the uses to which and for which the black people serve—both narrator and text—in a meditation on these matters.

One wonders what might signify the unlovely body in the story? The skin is coffee colored, but since that has no value acceptably repellant to the author, although it is to Mr. Head, there are other signifiers: the woman and the man are both fat and the woman's hair is unkempt. Fat and unkempt hair then are two such signals. And we know they are, for the two young women who accompany the fat colored man on the train are not described at all. One is in yellow, one in green, and they speak in "throaty" voices. O'Connor's black women are almost always in primary colors.

The climax of the story and the adventure is the encounter with a plaster nigger, not real flesh, and although we have been concentrating on the flesh of the body in the penetration of these Africanist characters as bodies of knowledge, it is important that the denial of his grandson is a denial of the head about the evil of its own body via the rejection of the body of his grandson.

The narrative turns at this point. This means by which unification takes place, by which forgiveness is possible, by which mercy arrives, by which self-respect is regained is via the transference of humiliation to a plastic black form and the clear evidence that self-loathing disappears once it is projected onto this plastic, artificial (invented, made, constructed, *built*) figure who, fortunately for the characters' requirements, is not alive and cannot speak, move, or, most importantly, *look*, return a look, or be understood to also *know* Mr. Head.

It is my contention that this story is paradigmatic and is an uncommonly explicit model of the way in which black characters function in fiction as a trope for (catalyst of) self-fabrication. Indeed the route to the fabricated self is dependent on a fabricated other, on the concept of othering. For if Mr. Head has no other, only aspects of the self that the self can choose to enter, the burden of genuine knowledge, genuine sight—like freedom—may be far too much to bear. Yet one wonders what the consequences would be. Suppose there were no *niggers* live or conveniently artificial for purposes of self-definition and self-approval if not self-love. Against the imposition of education-as-trauma there would be anarchy/chaos (racial education becomes a severance of the self and/or a denial of an aspect of the self that is vital). This trauma visited here on the male white child, and is followed by and dramatized by another incident of child abuse: (when the grandfather first deliberately fakes abandonment and then actually performs abandonment of the child to "teach him a lesson" in all senses of the word: the lesson being fear, dependence, isolation, distrust of anything outside "family/turf/tribe," and especially distrust of one's instincts, one's love, one's imagination, one's intellectual independence. It is this the grandfather hates in the boy and needs to stamp out) one's *connection* to *others*—all that is reduced or eliminated as part of the lesson, and the final lesson is a formulation of, separation of the self from the *body*—so it is not irrelevant that the grandfather's name is Mr. Head. Mind (knowledge, education) must win over the body (spirit, self-reliance, etc.).

Carson McCullers

I. ISOLATION AS MAN'S FATE

The principal theme of *The Heart Is a Lonely Hunter* (1940), Carson McCullers declared, lay in the first dozen pages: an individual's compulsion to revolt against enforced isolation and his or her urge to express the self at all costs. She thought of the work in 1938, even in one of its earliest forms in *The Mute,* as consisting of variations on this principal concept. Thinking of her projected novel as analogous to a work of music, she enumerated in her proposal to Houghton Mifflin five "counter-themes" that would, each of them, elaborate upon the central theme: the need for a person to create a unifying principle or god; the likelihood that any god that man creates will be chimerical or fantastic; the likely suppression by society of the individual; the deflection by social pressures of man's natural urge to cooperate with others; and the impressiveness of the heroism which occasionally appears in ordinary individuals. At times, these subsidiary themes would be obvious; at other times, they would be more difficult to define:

> These themes are never stated nakedly in the book. Their overtones
> are felt through the characters and situations. Much will depend

upon the insight of the reader and the care with which the book is read. In some parts the underlying ideas will be concealed far down below the surface of a scene and at other times these ideas will be shown with a certain emphasis.

When she wrote her abstract in 1938, she had completed Part I of the novel, had worked for over a year on the book, and had already made drastic changes in her central characters. A principal change from her projected plan is evident in the last section of the published novel. She had declared that, as with recurring motifs in a symphony, she would draw her major themes and all the counterthemes sharply together for an integrated finale. Actually, she did not do this.

Because her emphasis shifted as she worked on the novel, she gave greater importance by the end of the book to a young black woman, Portia Copeland, than she had first intended.

What is of interest here is the difference between what was planned (an integrated finale, and a minor character) and what was finally achieved. It may very well be that McCullers's serious and deeply probing gaze into her group of characters problematized her textual intentions precisely because she had not counted on, and had ultimately to take into consideration, the troubling presence of her African-American characters. What integration could have been possible among all of these Americans in the thirties when one of them was a fairly militant, certainly anarchic, intelligent, and complicated black man; when as an author she entered into his psyche; entered into his house; and provided him with a context *other* than the mainstream American definition, a focus inward as well as a sensitivity to the culture that arches over him. In short, her black Africanistic characters exist in time, in history. And since they do exist in time and in the contemporary social situation—they seem not to go quietly into any good night the author may have hoped to press them.

II. THE HEART IS A LONELY HUNTER

The author, female, white, Southern, twenty-two years old when the book is published, is writing in the late thirties. (Which is also the time period for Willa Cather, whose *Sapphira and the Slave Girl* was published in the same year. [?]) The thirties were the years of depressions and political upheavals. It was also the time of the first, certainly major, split between capitalism and communism in this country. (See Frank Kermode's *History and Value* for a description of it in England and a view of the war and political [poets]—for a similar thing happened in the States.) In any case, McCullers is to be commended for her sensitivity to these matters at such a tender age. With hindsight, we may at first find her novel—its organization—predictable: three outsiders in desperate need of a comrade and/or a community of like-minded intelligences, believe they have found such a friend when they meet and are befriended by John Singer. While no one of them has anything to say to the other, and while each is obsessive about his/her relationship with Singer, he barely understands what they are talking about and, himself, is desperate for the company of a moron—his "only friend." The friend without whom he cannot live, and does not.

Of the three, only Jake Blount seems to come out of nowhere—without family, birthplace, or a recognizable interior life that is anything other than his convictions and rage. He is described by others (and the author gives us enough details so that we might agree) as crazy. He certainly seems devoid of tenderness, incapable of personal relationships that are mutual, and gratitude. The same, the coldness and absence of tenderness, is true of Dr. Copeland. And if all three are obsessive including the girl Mick, we can understand the human rather than historical origins of their obsession. The marvel is how McCullers's efforts enter the body of the other and retreat from that body to provide alternate views of it. [Why no "resolution"?]

In *The Mortgaged Heart,* we learn that among her structural goals was this major one: that after the death of John Singer, the "quartet" that had deified him would come to understand him; that Biff would have his curiosity satisfied; that Mich would know something more about love and Singer; that Blount and Copeland would somehow come together—a gathering of desperate forces and people made necessary by the absence of the "god" they had singly invented. There is still the major note struck in the text that "no man should try it alone." It is put into the mouth of Dr. Copeland, and it may very well be that it is the presence of the black people in the book that thwarted McCullers's plan. It may be that her desire for harmony among these characters, harmony and resolution, at the end of the book is impossible because of the components of the confrontation she has constructed and the imaginative encounter that has taken place between the author and the Copeland family. Because this is her first novel, certain themes can be traced in the later ones, and the "resolutions" possible in the other books where there are no black characters would shed light on how much this first work predicted her later ones. How much the wrestle with ways in which black people confront a permanent alienation, permanent "dialogue with the deaf," influenced her later books. This dialogue with the deaf, for the Copelands, even Portia, is critical, because for them all white people are deaf. The singular thing about John for these Negroes is not that he cannot hear, but that he cannot speak. And not being able to speak means that *they* can; that there are spaces for their own speech, that there is little or no possibility of being rebuked, insulted, humiliated in words. And that their own words are not interrupted, dismissed, or patronized (although in fact Copeland is incomprehensible to Singer). For here is a white man without the power of hostile, dangerous, violent, and degrading language. In the case of Blount, Jake does not want anyone to answer him, he does not engage in dialogue—only monologue, and Singer is ideal for that purpose. With Mick, the urgency is for a sounding board, and after she loses the sounding board that is her brother (following his withdrawal as a result of her frightening him about the shooting accident) she is without anyone, any adult to whom she can speak about her inside room, and her plans. John Singer is the further door to music for her (he has a radio, and gives her full access to it). In all of their desires for the ultimate ally, whether the god of Portia and her grandfather, or the teacher Mick needs, or the "one who knows" that Jake needs, or the mirror image of the puzzling, mysterious "identity" that Biff needs (note the mirror passages with Biff, his looking at his face and seeing the "boundaries" of death), as well as Singer's own perfect love of the man he knows is his ultimate ally, it seems that only Dr. Copeland stands any chance of moral resurrection at the end. He, although reluctantly, returns to the protective haven of family and self providing communal living on the farm that the blacks own. The conversation with grandfather as he is carried away on the wagon intimates the possibility of dialogue, of communion. Note that Biff, Mick, and Jake are in almost complete solitude at the end. Only Dr. Copeland has the active, energetic love and acceptance of his family, and a real place of nourishment to go to. (See Margaret McDowell for a misreading of these endings—as well as a mistaken assumption that all of the post-Singer epiphanies are full of despair.)

The presence of the Copelands may have exploded McCullers's plans: for what "harmony" could there be in Georgia in 1939, the year before *Native Son* was published, between Copeland and the white characters in the text?

"Symbolic" and elliptical as her text is, it is still grounded in the stern social-realism of the late thirties. What could be more fake, more fantastical than a forced weaving of "understanding" of the people involved with Singer? It is impossible to postulate the mutual respect Blount and Jake can come to, the affection that could be on display between Mick and Copeland (it is already on display with him and Portia). And the attempt at reconciliation between Blount and Copeland could have taken place with a little tinkering. But with whom could Copeland, even if he came to his "senses," have had an adult, mutual relationship? Only with a child, who does not count, and a mute who is a kind of freak would any of it have lasted. For there would be no protection for any relationship that was planted.

Also there is an interesting, very modern component to the text. Their merging of identities and roles, although practically all of the criticism emphasizes the separateness, the isolation that is the root of these problems—there is an equally strong line of "joining" in it. The merging of gender in Biff Brannon, the merging of class among the blacks (the educated intellectual Dr. Copeland and his uneducated, religious family members). The maternal nature of Mick's father, the breadwinner role of her mother—it is she who manages. Only racial merging does not take place—in race the touch is confrontational or patronizing between blacks and whites. Against the background of insurmountable polarization is the foreground of edges drawn fuzzy, of the slip into the consciousness of an otherwise inaccessible place or other. "Proper place" is the overriding question. "Where and with whom do I belong?" the characters ask. "Nowhere," says Mick, in a foreign country, in an inside room. "Anywhere," says Jake, "so long as it is the South." "Among my people," says Copeland. "With Spires," says Singer. Biff does not ask: he is beyond the question. Only Copeland has a definite answer. Place for him is the fight to have one in the society at large, but to accomplish that, he attends to only his own people.

Also there are some interesting gaps. The mother of Mick—who has a role but no face or identity. Mick almost never thinks of her, seeks her company or advice, as she does her father. Her relationship with her own father, an inversion of the father/daughter relationship of Portia and her father. Where the white father is optimistic, incompetent, and for the purposes of "heading" the "household" worthless, he has nevertheless a strong paternal/maternal instinct. Copeland is very much the head and leader, owns his own brick home, is a physician, has professional colleagues, but has only the patriarchal instincts of a directorial head of household, of a community, as well as of a healer. Without the maternal or feminine elements he is solitary and disliked and feared. It is unusual to see this reversal in literature of two fathers, and it is unusual to see the relationship of father/daughter in which the black one is that mature, and the white one a child. Both Portia and Mick are motherless, and both have responsibilities with children (brothers). Portia worries about and writes to and supports and teaches Willie—worries herself into drinking at one point. Mick loves her brother but is able to "teach" him with terror, to punish him with threats of violence. But she is young. As a result he is cut off from her forever. Portia's "teachings" of mild acceptance don't do Willie much good but do provide a haven for him when the dire consequences have to be met. Copeland's response to crisis—confrontation—ends in worsened situations. Mr. Kelly's responses to crisis, the shooting of Baby, the illness of his daughter Etta, are primarily economic. A further burden imposed by the shooting, and the refusal to get medical help for Etta because there is no money. It is a strange and melancholy paradox, that the special but unnecessary medical comfort he is forced to pay for with Baby he assumes as his natural burden, but the medical help to save Etta is postponed and never, as far as we know, delivered. A further disturbing thought arises when we consider that Copeland could have and probably would have provided this help to Etta, if such could have been accepted by her and allowed by the organizations that regulate such things. It is never imagined or suggested by Portia or Mick or anyone.

There is another irony in the fact that Jake kills or believes he kills—he certainly is lying over the body of the one person who is as radical as he is: Lacy, the winner of the ambition Essay. And Lacy is the one person who is in fact taking serious instruction from Copeland.

Also the sexual encounter that Willie has leads to his irrevocable tragedy. The sexual encounter that Mick has leads to almost nothing—except the flight of her friend who is full of self-reprisal for the act for both sexual and religious reasons. There is no other sexual encounter in the text, but a great deal of sexual implication: the homosexual personality of Biff; the asexual but nevertheless volup-

tuous yearnings of Singer; the sex-as-weakness relationship of Copeland with his wife. There is no woman at all in Jake's life or even in
his memory.

Also each and every "isolated" character has had a memorable
attempt at group-making: Jake actually formed a group but was outraged when they used their treasury to buy human vulnerable organi-
zational things [*sic*]: hats and beer. Copeland gave regular lectures at
his Christmas party, and formed his family, or tried to, into a "cell."
Mick has a party to which she invites all of the "best" people at her
school. It ends in disarray, although quite exciting disarray that she
joins, but she does not develop one single friendship out of the affair.
(And her other coupling ends with a handshake and a postcard saying
OK.) Her only other attempt at a group or community is the urgent
one of an orchestra—which may never be realized now, or, one feels,
just might. John Singer meets a group, a collection of other mutes,
too late—when he has learned of Spires's death, and is not able to take
advantage of their camaraderie and acceptance. Biff's group is made
up of the customers in his restaurant, and the exceptional kindnesses
he makes available to the "hurt" ones. His attempts are "successful"
because he demands so little from them. He is the needy one.

Some concluding observations re: *Heart*

1. The language. Copeland's formal enunciation isolates
   him—his family speaks another language/idiom, and neither
   rubs off on the other. Why? McCullers gives Portia's speech
   a special "Negro" syntax that is different from uneducated
   whites. Note how Simms speaks. Where is the nominative
   used as the subjective voice in any other person's speech?
   What are the inconsistencies, if any, in Portia's and Willie's
   speech?
2. The style of prose describing Negro houses. Copeland's is
   exceptional, but we are never in Portia's house, are we? When
   is she lyric? When didactic? When naturalistic? Fableistic?

Harriet Beecher Stowe

O'Connor and McCullers are able to employ and rely on previous and well-established codes in Africanist discourse for the powerful resonances that discourse provides in stressing difference or destabilizing it.

One major literary matrix which shaped and informed, just as it was itself shaped and informed by these discursive practices, is Harriet Beecher Stowe's *Uncle Tom's Cabin*. In that novel, mid-nineteenth-century readers and late twentieth-century readers can find the fundamental argument for and architecture of the separation of the races. This separation, however, follows abolition in Miss Stowe's novel; and it is a separation that rests on the novel's dedication to proving similarity. But the strategies of separateness are nevertheless the program. We are invited to enter the minds, hearts, lives, and houses of slaves as well as slaveholders to learn what in fact must be sundered and what must be put asunder. Slavery must be sundered—that is the goal and purpose of the work. White and black must be put asunder, separated—that is H. B. Stowe's solution to the problem of the residual Africanist presence that slavery leaves in its wake.

The terms of the contract issued by the author—a contract to which the reader becomes party—are visible at once. In the title, the table of contents, and the Preface. If we imagine ourselves as white mid-nineteenth-century readers, the title indicates the protagonist is our friend, is someone we need not fear or distrust because he is *like an uncle,* if not truly an uncle. He is an affectionate adult of no status other than, perhaps, age. His status as beneath the reader's, or if the reader is a child, *equal* to the reader's, is signaled by the absence of two markers: Mr. and a surname. He is Tom and we need not fear, respect, or take him seriously—if we don't want to—but we are encouraged to make his acquaintance, be in his company because he is friendly—like an uncle. But not a fierce uncle with some power over us, but an uncle without the status of living in or owning a house; this is an uncle who lives in a cabin. It might occur to us that this cabin is a vacation accommodation, or a getaway, but it is not an idea that holds us for long because the subtitle removes any doubt about that: Life Among the Lowly. All of these signs are important principally because of the void created by the deliberate erasure of the two words that signify the theme, the content, the purpose, the strategy of the novel: slave and black. Neither slavery nor race surfaces explicitly in the title or subtitle and that is our first clue of the project Harriet Beecher Stowe has undertaken.

Further erasures, even more pointed, are to be found in the table of contents—a listing that leads us from one set of altered assumptions to another. I say "altered" because in 1852, the date of the publication, white American authors, white American people, seldom failed (if in fact they ever failed) to limit an Africanist persona to his or her race or status in relation to slavery. This was the period during which terms like coon, darky, nigger were part of printed and published titles. The period when the word "Negro" (like "black" with a capital letter) was a term of respect hard-won by Africanist people themselves.

This novel, serialized between June 1851 and April 1852 in *National Era* magazine, does not make any reference in its chapter titles to slave until chapter 30. All references to slavery before chapter 30 are shifted to the term "property," "living property." That shift is a gesture to impress upon us the outrage, or paradox of owning another human being. "Showing the Feelings of Living Property on Changing Owners"; "The Property Is Carried Off"; "In Which Property Gets into an Improper State of Mind." In chapter 30, however, the word "slave" is used to buttress one of Miss Stowe's most persuasive arguments: abolition of slavery is necessary because of the horrors of the slave warehouse. Following that chapter heading, she uses another powerfully evocative term, "The Middle Passage." This phrase, normally confined in its usage to mean the trip of kidnapped Africans on slave ships to the New World, she employs for its associative values to the journey from one slave master to another; from a benevolent master to an abusive one. Not from freedom (Africa) to bondage, but from kindness to savagery; from a Christian household to a depraved one. And the disembarkation at the end of this "middle passage" is chapter 32, entitled "Dark Places." In addition to trying to reverse and alter certain resistant contemporaneous assumptions by a deferment of the term "slave," the substitution of the term "Living Property"; and no explicit mention of race in these titles until *after* "the middle passage" and "dark places," when Cassy is given a full narrative and identified as a quadroon—in addition to these careful choices, there is another perhaps more and certainly equally significant choice. The co-protagonists of the novel, Eliza and George, also slaves, also Africanist, are introduced in chapter headings as mother, father, husband. These terms are designed to remove, annihilate "slavery" from our perception and our intimate view of this couple before reassigning it to them. The effort is to make the assignment of the meaning of "slave" to them (Eliza and George) preposterous, outrageous, and unequivocally evil. The preposterousness of the equation Eliza and slave / George and slave is gained by descriptions of them as not just graceful, virtuous, etc., but also because they are beautiful and in their bodies, similar to white people. What then is truly outrageous is that the reader is forced to consider her- or himself in that very position.

Stowe explodes the possibility of "othering." The mother or father or husband reading the book (presumed to be white) is now reading about not an alien but another mother, father, or husband who is physically *like* him or her and may even be as virtuous as he or she is.

After the serialization in *National Era,* as the edition was being prepared for publication in two volumes, Miss Stowe wrote a preface that further binds the reader even to the terms of her contract—guiding and legislating entrance into her novel. Simply put, the Preface clarifies the purpose of the work, deflects the possibility of white readers feeling threatened by this entrance into an Africanist space, or feeling any guilt about the fact that the space exists all. The message of the Preface is that THERE IS SAFETY FOR WHITE PEOPLE AND SELF-APPROVAL AS WELL IN THE FREEING OF THE SLAVES.

[*Explicate the Preface*]

The terms of the contract the author has issued to us, and to which we accede for the purpose of reading, are enforced and embellished by the methods the author employs to lead the reader into what the title promises: an inside view of Tom's cabin, a view of Africanist space; the domestic and domesticated heart of darkness. And once we understand the preposterousness of the reader's look-alike or feel-alike, of being a slave (in chapters 1–3), we can safely enter (in chapter 4) the read territory, the very black space—the locus of the slave's interior—his cabin.

In chapter 4 we note first the description of the external landscape of Tom's cabin—a description that, like the later description of Simon Legree's house, sets the stage for what we will find inside. [*READ*]

Note further the delay of this entrance, the entrance proper, until it is safe. Signs of safety are the nurturing, the bounty, and the accommodation. Following these moorings comes another: the script, the written language, the master's text that the protagonist is attempting to learn. [*READ*]

The final anchor or mooring that provides safety and protection for the reader into this mysterious or forbidding Africanist darkness is the presence of a white guide. It is he who speaks the first word of dialogue in this chapter and who, by initiating speech, permits and releases the blacks to speak also. It is important, however, if we are to hear what Stowe wants us to believe is natural, unpoliced, realistic Africanist speech, speech delivered to be intimate and unselfconscious, accurate and faithful, that the white person initiating and encouraging this speech must be a child. Although completely misunderstood, Dr. Copeland's dialogue with Jake is remarkable because it is the first dialogue we have read between white and black adults except for Ishmael and Queequeg.

Young master George becomes the reader's point of reference. A good deal of this chapter, Tom's effort to learn to write notwithstanding, is about nourishment—food. Aunt Chloe's pride in her cooking, her susceptibility to the arousal of feelings of competition regarding other cooks in the neighborhood, but particularly this young boy's position of comfort, privilege, and power, along with his nourishment in this cabin. It is he for whom Aunt Chloe is cooking with special care; it is he who tosses bits of food (the way you throw scraps to pets) to her children; it is he who orders this adult, this woman, this other mother, to make some cake for her own children.

Following the establishment of these power and nurturing relationships is a religious meeting in which George participates. This meeting is not the account McCullers provides in which there are no whites to interpret for the reader, or to verify and witness the scene. This meeting is safe for the reader because of the white person's presence; his gaze is operative and his participation forgivable because he is a child. There is a triad here of education, nourishment, and religion, carefully built into the chapter to make its ending more horrific: for the end is the violent assault on the promise of the triad. We learn that nurturing, education-hungry, religious Tom is indeed being sold to the unpleasant slave trader we were introduced to in chapter 1. The exploration of two points (at least two) enables us to complicate and analyze Stowe's project. One is the context she provides for the slaves—giving them a family context, an historical context, and an interior life—some parts of which we have touched on already. The other is the context of the novel.

It might be useful to know something of the appetite for published slave narratives to which *Uncle Tom's Cabin* contributed. And the place these narratives had in the Abolitionist Movement. *Equiano or Gustavas Vassa, the African, Written by Himself,* published in 1769, had thirty-six editions between that date and 1850. Frederick Douglass's *Narrative of the Life of Frederick Douglass, an American Slave, Written by Himself,* published in 1845, sold five thousand copies in four months, and eleven thousand by 1847. Henry Bibb's *Narrative of the Life and Adventures of Henry Bibb, an American Slave, Written by Himself,* was published in 1849. Charles Bell's *Life and Adventures of a Fugitive Slave* appeared in 1836 in the *Quarterly Anti-Slavery Magazine.* Josiah Henson's *Narrative* sold five thousand copies before publication. (This narrative being the one upon which Miss Stowe is believed to have based much of her characterization of Uncle Tom.) Moses Roper's *Narrative* had ten editions from 1837 to 1856. William Wells Brown's story was reprinted four times in its first year. Solomon Northrup's *Twelve Years a Slave* sold twenty-seven thousand copies in two years.

The publishing history of slave women's narratives is different, troubled, even, but from the dictated story of Mary Prince (a West Indian woman), examined and approved of by her editor (Pringle) and published as a tract by him in 1831 in London, through Harriet Jacobs's (Linda Brent's) *Incidents in the Life of a Slave Girl,* published in 1861, there were ample representations of slave women's narratives, although they were not understood to have the same force or be as persuasive as male narratives—unable or unwilling as female narratives were to describe a solitary, do-it-alone journey from slavery to *manhood,* and heavily dependent as they were on community help and the imposed restrictions and assumed obligations of children and family. In addition, and this is significant for our understanding of Stowe's handling of Eliza and Cassy, the horror of slavery for African-ist women was frequently understood not to be enslavement—unless it was inconvenient for their mates or husbands—but sexual abuse. (I can't go any further into these personal thoughts and editorializing, but you may wish to in your precepts.) In any case, to quote from one critic, "no slave society wrote more or meditated more or said more about its condition than African and African-American slaves." *Uncle Tom's Cabin,* therefore, is not like Topsy; it had parents and it knew their names.

In that milieu, the same one Herman Melville lived in, the milieu of abolitionism, pro-slavery forces, Free Soil debates, the Fugitive Slave Law, and threats and forebodings of war, Harriet Beecher Stowe's novel can be seen as what Lincoln described as "the book that started this great war." It can also be seen simply as heavy propaganda, ameliorating and altering raw racist assumptions, as a grossly senti-mentalized account of American life vis-à-vis Africanism—a number of other strengths and weaknesses attributable to it. I think these credits and charges are worth some discussion, but I would like to add the points I touched upon a moment ago about context—the way in which the *context* into which the book places the slaves—a family and historical context—is also the context in which class formulations, white supremacy, and racial separation were raised, embellished, and sanctioned.

Uncle Tom's Cabin bridges and collapses the class problems for both Southern Democrat and Northern Republican by an appeal to a unified and unifying concept of the evils of slavery, to wit: *good* slaveowners are good to their slaves and are simply trapped by the sys-tem of slavery—not racism; *good* slaveowners are well born, and if by chance not, they are nevertheless moral. *Bad* slaveowners are ill-bred and/or shrewd, uneducated, lascivious, un-Christian. *Good* north-erners, slave-owning or abolitionist, are well-born, moral, Christian, industrious, etc. The division between good and bad, Christian and un-Christian, mannered and unmannered, hides the class division that was erupting all over the country. These class conflicts surface explicitly in the novel, but disappear when one considers that the true abomination and cause of regional and economic strife is the slave system that is an abomination to *everybody except* the kind of people who exist in every class—the immoral or un-Christian and the unaesthetic. [*READ pp. chapter 1, the slave trader, and chapter 31 and ff. of Simon Legree.*]

But there is an interesting formula, a surefire spectacle which can be relied upon to unify and join the slave trader and the slave owner; to join Haley of the terrible tie and Mr. Shelby. An interesting figuration that unites St. Clare and Miss Ophelia whose views on slavery are oppositional if not adversarial. It is even a figuration which joins Simon Legree to his own slaves. This is the figure of *Jim Crow.*

In the very first scene of chapter 1, we learn of the marked differences in class, education, and piety between Haley and Mr. Shelby. [*READ the information provided in the first three comments Haley makes.*] If his clothes and manner were not instructive enough, these comments alone would theatricalize the class differences. The unification between them, however, the moment of mutual shared agreement and delight, comes when Eliza's child enters the room. The very first words Mr. Shelby speaks to him are "Hulloa, Jim Crow!" [*READ p. 13*] Further, in chapters 19 and 20, we are treated first to the discussion of the pros and cons of slavery, class, etc., after which there enters a figure, a *thing,* called Topsy, who after being spoken of is spoken *to* with the same invitation Mr. Shelby made to Eliza's son: "I thought she was rather a funny specimen in the *Jim Crow* line. Here, Topsy," he added, giving a whistle, as a man would to call the attention of a dog, "give us a song, now, and show us some of your dancing." . . . "and the thing struck up, in a clear, shrill voice, an odd negro melody, to which she kept time with her hands and feet, spinning round, clapping her hands, knocking her knees together, in a wilde, fantastic sort of time, and producing in her throat all those *odd guttural sounds which distinguish the native music of her race;* and finally, turning a summerset or two, and giving a prolonged closing note, as odd and unearthly as that of a steam-whistle, she came suddenly down on the carpet, and stood with her hands folded . . ." (p. 279) [*Add Topsy's characteristics*]

Simon Legree, a New Englander, of modest if not poor background, who ran off to sea at an early age to seek his fortunes there since he had none at home, who emulated his "hard-tempered sire," who threw his entreating mother "senseless on the floor," who "carouses with drunken sailors," a coarse man, rapist, atheist, greedy, who is able to increase both his self-esteem and his pocket because of the slave system—he also responds to a budding conscience, a slight recognition of sin with another version of the Jim Crow figure. After his fright at the curl of hair presented to him which reminds him of his metaphorical matricide, he calls his dogs to keep him company. When they won't, he makes the other choice for comfort and reconciliation: "I'll have Sambo and Quimbo up here, to sing and dance one of their hell dances, and keep off these horrid notions." ". . . after warming them up with whiskey, [he liked to] amuse himself by setting them to singing, dancing or fighting, as the humor took him." (A description memorable for its echo in *Absalom, Absalom!*) Simon Legree *joins* his Jim Crows in "shrieking, whooping . . . singing and making all manner of ludicrous and horrid grimaces at each other." (pp. 435–436)

Alexander Saxton's article on blackface minstrelsy, which is also a chapter in his book, *The Rise and Fall of the White Republic*, argues that blackface minstrelsy—as an early formulation of mass media through its theatrical/entertainment accessibility—enforced racism, appropriated Africanist music for the purposes of such enforcement, and provided the paradox of whites able to speak illegal radical thoughts, thoughts, and opinions considered socially unacceptable and politically inflammatory. The dual serviceability of Africanism released contradictory forces (the use of a confining black mask to experience license and freedom; appropriation *and* degradation of the Africanist culture for purposes of delight). He also argues how minstrelsy created (his words are "propagandized metaphorically") alliances between the planter class and the urban working class; between the planter class and the rural and small-town populace. [*READ p. 165*]

The "urban" feel, the identification with a coherent *national* platform; a *national* view of Africanism all seem to have been at the heart of Mark Twain's excitement, for, as Mr. Saxton observes, he would have seen slaves dancing and singing in his own hometown. In some terribly powerful way, minstrelsy united regions, city and town, rural and urban, and *all classes* of whites could gaze upon a burgeoning Americanness taking place, and the spectacle of plastic blacks, "artificial niggers," constituted Africanistic discourse *freely* voicing white fears, apprehensions, and sexual yearnings. All of which take place in the era of Jacksonian democracy, advancing parochial notions of the Democratic party, and ultimately enshrining Republican party, even Whiggish notions of the Republic.

Part of Stowe's project is to subsume class under the cloak of black slavery; the major utility of minstrelsy is to unify class from behind the mask of racism. Both are signaled by the figuration of Jim Crow—the dance and the name stolen and appropriated by the man credited with its invention. Thus the *context* into which the novel places the slaves (beloved, beautiful sons; funny specimens of "thing" without parents; or brutish and brutalized black drivers) is also the context in which class formulations, white supremacy, and racial separation were raised, embellished, and sanctioned.

There is also a larger context which can help us think through this novel. In addition to the elusive, shifting merging of class interests, *Uncle Tom's Cabin* also melts law and culture, turning both into a heady brew of feeling. Feelings which are summoned for their veracity and universality but which are subjective, unanalytical, and, as has been suggested, ideological as well. This is the function and recourse of the realistic and sentimental novel.

In a chapter called "The Law of the Heart," Terry Eagleton has a couple of things (at least) to say that are instructive here. Tracing ethics, reason, and aesthetics, he observes, in regard to Shaftesbury, that "his [Shaftesbury's] unity of ethics and aesthetics, virtue and beauty, is most evident in the concept of manners. Manners for the eighteenth century signify that meticulous disciplining of the body which converts morality to style, deconstructing the opposition between the proper and the pleasurable. In these regulated forms of civilized conduct, a pervasive aestheticizing of social practices gets under way: moral imperatives no longer impose themselves with the leaden weight of some Kantian duty, but infiltrate the very textures of lived experience as tact or know-how, intuitive good sense or inbred decorum."

> Legal, political and economic transformations must therefore be translated into new forms of unthinking social practice, which in a kind of creative repression or amnesia can come to forget the very conventions they obey . . . Structures of power must become structures of feeling; and the aesthetic is a vital mediation in this shift from property to propriety. . . .
>
> If the aesthetic comes in the eighteenth century to assume the significance it does, it is because the word is shorthand for a whole project of hegemony, the massive introjection of abstract reason by the life of the senses . . . It would thus ideally be as inconceivable for the subject to violate the injunctions of power as it would be to find a putrid odour enchanting . . .
>
> The moment when moral actions can be classified chiefly as "agreeable" or "disagreeable," when these aesthetic terms will do service for more complex distinctions, marks a certain mature point of evolution in the history of a social class. Once the dust and heat

of its struggles for political power have subsided, moral questions which were at that time necessarily cast in stridently absolutist terms may now be allowed to crystallize into routine response. Once new ethical habits have been installed and naturalized, the sheer quick feel or impression of an object will be enough for sure judgment, short-circuiting discursive contention and thus mystifying the rules which regulate it. If aesthetic judgment is every bit as coercive as the most barbarous law—for there is a right and wrong to taste quite as absolute as the death sentence—this is not at all the way it feels . . .

If one wished to name the most important cultural instrument of this hegemony in the nineteenth century, one which never ceases to grasp universal reason in concretely particular style, uniting within itself an economy of abstract form with the effect of lived experience, one might do worse than name the realist novel . . .

Quoting Franco Moretti, Eagleton goes on:

It is not enough that the social order is "legal"; it must also appear symbolically legitimate . . . It is also necessary that, as a "free individual," not as a fearful subject but as a convinced citizen, one perceives the social norms as *one's own*. One must internalize them and fuse external compulsion and internal impulse into a new unit until the former is no longer distinguishable from the latter.

The growing aestheticization of social life, then, represents a major hegemonic advance on the part of the governing bloc.

"Sensibility" seems at once the surest foundation, and no foundation at all.

Harriet Beecher Stowe capitalizes on these aesthetics—imploring us to trust our feelings and the pleasure that goodness brings. Her notions of beauty (acceptable color, manners, dress) are imposed on the reader as universal and as natural. When physical aesthetics are not available to her (as with Uncle Tom, as with Topsy, Chloe, and so on) she has immediate access to a morality which mitigates the absence of bodily beauty. This morality is Christianity. And under the umbrella of Christian virtue, virtue *is* beauty; and "whitens" whatever blackness there is. In fact, like minstrelsy, virtue or symbolic "whiteness" is more dramatic if housed in a black face.

Eva, of course, is the apotheosis of beauty and virtue—so perfectly melded the book cannot sustain the glow without immolating itself. Among the many reliefs in the novel, her death is surely the most welcome. But Eliza and George have few rivals among the adult characters, and because Tom is and cannot be physically attractive—since he has no white blood to alleviate his color—his Christian virtue has no peer other than the first Christian, Christ Himself. To Whom he is frequently compared.

I said, earlier, that Stowe provides these Africanist characters with a *historical* as well as family context. That historical context is Africa, and her urgings and her solutions to the problems pursuant to the African presence in the States is emigration for them all. For the quadroon, and the mulatto and the very black skinned, not a search for a past, not a search for a culture they might have some connection to, but a search, in the truest American sense, for a future. Africa is not so much "home" as an opportunity for further missionary work; that is where George and his family, and Topsy (once rehabilitated) go.

Throughout the novel Stowe has emphasized the violence of slavery, brutality to the body and to the finer senses. Violence is immoral and unaesthetic. Violence that is systemic and which crosses class lines and erases its tracks, leaving racisms alone as God's divisions, God's hierarchical organization of the human race. With that alteration in the nature of things, Miss Stowe will have nothing to do.

Mark Twain

Our reading of Harriet Beecher Stowe's *Uncle Tom's Cabin* focused on the development of a narrative which is almost solely *dependent on context* for understanding both in its own time and in ours. Stowe can be said to be both acknowledging the ideology and assumptions of her time and making an effort to alter them. Our contemporary reading necessarily takes the novel's *historicity* into account for even the most superficial reading, but also looks at the *implications of history* on the technique of novel writing.

In our papers and analyses, however, we must refrain from resting the case on documentary readings. That is, do them, consider the ideological framework, the historical and social set in which the work is placed and in which it was written, but because we are interested in the *self-reflexive* properties, the even narcissistic nature of these white/black engagements, the merely documentary will not do. Such readings cannot fully explore or identify *parody, irony, or significant silences, evasions, or speech which may counter or quarrel with the "outside the text" documentary material.* We do not want to "reinsert a text into its empirical context but indicate how a text responds to its context."

There are three ways of reading a novel's response to the Africanistic presence it encounters: symptomatic, critical or contestatory, and transformational. These are not always separate and always boundaried categories. Rather they are tendencies which shape the relationship of the text to its context. Frequently they overlap and provide a supplementary reading that invites a documentary understanding but is not limited to it.

In searching for instances where the above three ways of reading can be discovered, we should note (a) instances where Africanistic space is entered [x]; (b) where Africanistic bodies come in contact (other than rape or violence) with a white body; and (c) whether and how interchanges between the two (white and black characters) are ethical moments or have ethical implications [x]. That is, whether the black character is being judged morally and how that judgment is a reflection of the white's own values (Marie, for example, in the "honeymoon" episode in Havana, and her inquiry about "wenches" [*To Have and Have Not*]); and whether the white uses the judgment as an opportunity to react ethically. (Kindness, for example, to an "undeserving" black would privilege the white's moral posture, as in Hemingway.)

Supplementary readings can be those in which the form of the novel wages war with its own content (*Absalom, Absalom!*) in a declared war, or in undeclared war when the form collapses under the weight of its inadequately problematized content (Styron). It is very interesting when we find in the work an unconscious and traumatic rupture with the past and/or the present, and in which the individual is put on trial, questioning the context, reacting to the rage and impotence of the bourgeoisie, discovering the instability of the self in relation to external or internalized "others," and possibly through this process, the narrative acts as an especially incisive critique of moral, ideological, and cultural aspects of its world. If we keep in mind the place of *fiction in history and history in fiction* (how the novel comes to terms with "pertinent contexts and what political implications such as 'coming to terms' may arguably have," we see how a "text may . . .

render its contexts in critical and potentially transformative ways that close reading may disclose."

These points are especially helpful in the reading of *Huckleberry Finn.*

Now, we are still under the syllabus heading of *The Visible Other as Idiom,* and, as we saw with *Uncle Tom's Cabin,* the black body or bodies are being marked and stratified or privileged by color. Stowe's novel is an example of sharing characteristics with the colors— the visibleness—of Africanistic personnel. That is, she demarcates color, flags it, and employs it to further the reader's identification or to manipulate it. She does this by transferring the narrator's, the assumed reader's, values and customs to and within the seeable, visible (meaning markedly, visibly different) other. In such a transfer, the less visibly different (the light-skinned) are permitted more play, more aggression, more empowerment, more militancy than those whose visible difference is extreme. This latter must have *sharable* traits as theatrical and as pronounced and as singularly "pure" as his or her color difference. The extremely visible character, Tom, thereby becomes a saint of incredible, even despicable, proportions, or a villain equally outsized. [x] It is as though the inherent cultural critique in which Stowe engages requires these powerful signs of transfer and repression because the culture is so resistant to critique it needs the largest possible weapons to surrender.

Further trait-sharing is accomplished when the Africanistic characters are put into a family context, and given a language (becoming speaking blacks, thinking, contemplating blacks). Their speech, their interior thoughts, however, rendered according to ideological protocol, empower them to a certain extent in the work (in a way that Poe does not, and in a way that Melville does not in *Moby-Dick* because of the p.v. [point of view]), and empower the reader to a great extent to continue the critique in his or her own mind.

Alternatively, in Twain, we see the critique disguised as, or enhanced by, humor and naivete. And the color or visible signs are more or less absent. The demarcation is not color, but the institution of slavery versus the possibilities of freedom. (There are references to "yaller gals" and there seems to be the assumption that Jim can be easily identified from the shore, but there is no flagging of color.) Because of the combination of humor and the naif, Twain's reader is free to dismiss the critique, the contestatory qualities of the novel.

> The romantic side of Tom Sawyer is shown in most delightfully humorous fashion in the account of his difficult devices to aid in the easy escape of Jim, a runaway negro. Jim is an admirably drawn character. There have been not a few fine and firm portraits of negroes in recent American fiction, of which Mr. Cable's Bras-Coupe in the *Grandissimes* is perhaps the most vigorous, and Mr. Harris's Mingo and Uncle Remus and Blue Dave are the most gentle. Jim is worthy to rank with these; and the essential simplicity and kindliness and generosity of the Southern negro have never been better shown than here by Mark Twain.
>
> They have one great charm, all of them—they are not written about and about; they are not described and dissected and analyzed; they appear and play their parts and disappear; and yet they leave a sharp impression of indubitable vitality and individuality. No one, we venture to say, who reads this book will readily forget the Duke and the King, a pair of as pleasant 'confidence operators' as one may meet in a day's journey, who leave the story in the most appropriate fashion, being clothed in tar and feathers and ridden on a rail. Of the more broadly humorous passages—and they abound—we have not left ourselves space to speak; they are to the full as funny as in any of Mark Twain's other books . . .

These reviews missed or dismissed the social quarrel in the novel because the work (a) appears to be symptomatic (that is, the novel assimilates and inscribes the ideological assumptions of its society and culture), (b) is narrated in a voice and with a gaze of a child-without-status (that is, someone outside, marginal, and already "othered" by the middle class society he loathes and seems never to envy), and (c) masks itself in the comic, the parodic, the exaggerated believe-me-or-not tone. All three of these features are dependent on an already-legislated response to the racial idiom in which Africanistic presences are placed.

The novel assimilates its contemporary attitudes toward black slaves and is therefore symptomatic of those attitudes, thereby deluding the reader into a false sense of stability. The narrator's gaze and voice belong to a witty, what we would now call street-smart, but hostilely uneducated young boy enthralled, initially, by romance, childhood for its own sake and value, and uncorrupted by middle-class respectability and fury. [x] On this young innocent, Twain, the legislator, inscribes the critique of slavery and the pretensions of the would-be middle class, the resistance to loss of Eden and the difficulty of becoming that "oxymoron a social individual." The agency, however, for Huck's struggle is the nigger, Jim, and it is absolutely necessary (for the reasons stated above) that the term "nigger" be inextricable from Huck's deliberations about who and what he himself is. Or more precisely, is not. As a matter of fact, some of the major controversies about the "greatness" or near greatness of *Huck Finn* as an American (or even "world") novel exist as controversies because they lack a close examination of the interdependency of slavery and freedom, of Huck's growth and Jim's serviceability within it, and even of Twain's inability to continue, explore the journey into free territory, and the collapse of the so-called "fatal" ending of the novel.

But before we discuss the Evasion, the ending of *Huckleberry Finn* upon which so much seems to rest regarding whether the novel is understood, and understood to be "great" / "great American" / "great world" novel, or badly flawed . . . before I make any comments on that, we should examine the speech, the silence in the novel, and how each contributes to the moral empowerment at the heart of the book.

Twain provides us, a modern audience, with the same opportunity for meditating on these problems that Huck is provided with and we are not, nor is Huck, allowed to continue that meditation without Jim's *informing, mutating presence.*

In previous lectures we have considered literature in which the African was positioned as "other" and employed as an enabling device—an agent for identifying what the narrator/character is not (or is). We understand what the eccentric LeGrand is or is not by his favorable comparison to the nameless or named black characters around him: virile, stoic, self-reliant in one novel. We are made to understand what illicit, illegal "devil"-like sensuality is by his use of Africanistic tropes in *The Garden of Eden.* We understand what kind of man Ishmael is by his sometimes favorable, sometimes unfavorable comparison to Queequeg. In Melville's work the Africanist characters become learning opportunities, opportunities to contemplate one's own self and one's own civilization. Melville's agenda is less programmatic than Poe's, or Hemingway's or even Stowe's. The Africanistic presence becomes more complicated, and in Willa Cather, Carson McCullers, and Flannery O'Connor this presence is decidedly problematized. What has surface simplicity in Hemingway becomes impossible to sustain in *Sapphira and the Slave Girl* and *The Heart Is a Lonely Hunter.* The complicated, yet useful, process of "othering" for purposes of self-definition is explicit in *The Artificial Nigger* and *Everything That Rises Must Converge.*

We should remember that one of the major conveniences of this particular kind of "othering" is his visibility—his blackness. Several kinds of foreigners, heretics, aliens have been fabricated in cultures throughout history, of course. And the process of identifying the foreigner is a careful one. Sometimes the heretic or foreigner is perceived as out there, away, beyond the border deserving righteous wrath or earning missionary conversion. Sometimes this heretic or foreigner is within: within the state, the family, the self. Whether away or within, the foreigner's foreignness must be identified if it is to be rooted out, contained, or altered and absorbed. Whole systems of codes are developed to make this identification. Think for example of what witchcraft was: the intimate, interior presence of the alien (one's sister, neighbor, friend, mother, aunt, uncle, etc.). The methods for determining witchhood, and for the expulsion of that particular kind of sinister "other." No such complicated pattern of identification has been needed for Africans and African-Americans because the visibility was so marked. The greater threat was that one "could not tell," thus the prohibition against racial mixing, the horror of learning that one had black blood and so on. So here one has the advantage of a visible other. And what can happen, and what I believe did happen, was that this visible other came to be seen as available for explorations into language, speech, silence, literary language, and oral speech. Language as class distinction; language as empowerment. Into language as American rather than English.

Another availability taken advantage of was the employment of the visible other's character. Addressing the lingering over his or her body and personality—the way it looked, what passion, legal or illicit, it was prey to, what pain it could endure, what limits there were to suffering, what possibilities there were to forgiveness, to compassion, to love. When we read *Uncle Tom's Cabin* and *Huckleberry Finn,* two things strike us: the apparently limitless store of love and compassion the blacks have for their white masters, and the assumption that the whites are indeed what they say they are—superior and adult. This representation of the visible other can be read as yearning, desire for forgiveness and love—but that yearning is made possible only when it is understood that the "other" had indeed *recognized his foreignness and despised it.* Like the witch who is proven to be normal by being thrown into the water and sinking to its bottom like a normal person would—and thereby drowning—the Africanistic character must recognize the value of admiring and joining his persecutors—though it may kill him, and culturally speaking does kill him. The Africanistic "other" also offers an opportunity to dwell on gender roles and differences. Not merely the virility of men, but the vulnerability of women. Their power and powerlessness, their sexuality, their social responsibilities, and especially the threat they represent—seduction, rage, judgment. And in this way it becomes important to "know" them as women and as other. But this knowledge, posited as it is on the fabrication of a locus of evil in order to know and thereby control it, is necessarily one-sided. The witch, the foreigner, the black, *the other has nothing to say.* Or, if so, nothing to say that one is bound to listen to and consider its truth. What we should be looking for, then, in *Huckleberry Finn* (and in *Uncle Tom's Cabin* and in *Three Lives*) is when are the Africanistic characters allowed to speak and what do they say. Is what they say a part of the author's "knowing" and thereby controlling the black character? Is this speech a disruption in the text, a transformation, a contestation? We should do a close reading of the talking and sharing through speech that Huck and Jim do. This is the exchange that makes for the friendship upon which all of Huck's moral struggles ride.

We can divide up the speech and silences into three categories, although there are more, each of which helps clarify Huck's growth, Huck's self-meditation.

1. What and how does Huck learn of kindness and love?
2. How Huck struggles with and resolves his struggle with ethics versus institutional religion.
3. How Huck defines "freedom" and what it comes to mean to him.

I. KINDNESS AND LOVE

This is an important quest because all Huck seems to be acquainted with are Miss Watson and his father, Pap, both of whom, in symbolic and literal ways, are trying to kill him; one by "pecking," giving him stories of damnation, squeezing all joy from life; the other by trying to take his flesh and blood life, by using him for greedy and criminal purposes.

Much of Huck's quest for kindness and love, which is also a parallel quest to be kind, and *to love,* is worked out with Jim. In two ways. Encounters with Jim and the speech and silence they share.

Encounters

p. 10 Huck refuses to tie Jim and Tom wishes him to

p. 19 Huck goes to Jim (not Tom) when in a serious crisis for magical powers and prophecy.

p. 37 Huck happy to see him, though Jim fearful he is a ghost

p. 38 "ever so glad . . . I warn't *lonesome.*" Huck assumes role of provider.

p. 71 Huck is the object of Jim's love and grief. Following this scene, Huck is sorry for drunks in circus. p. 119

Speech and shared silences

pp. 41ff Huck is dominator—shown to be smarter than Jim

p. 54 exchange of information—as equals

p. 55 shared silence: ripe, lyric, and intimate

p. 56 balancing

pp. 64–65 royalty discussion—Jim outspoken

p. 77 exchange of information and *shared* plans—as equals

p. 97 another shared silence when they are naked, meditative, intimate, harmonious, etc.

p. 125 between chs. 23–24, a strange silence, a kind of interchapter hiatus, more pregnant than all of the silences because it is never followed up. "Next day . . ." Also this monologue of Jim's revealing his interior thoughts and his family life outside his relation to Huck's is preceded by a critique of royalty (p. 124). And followed by (a) Jim's being tied up in the wigwam and (b) turned into a *sick Arab,* harmless and docile or crazy. In between the critique of aristocracy, the class contempt for the pretensions of the upper class and the condition of Jim as roped and bound slave or minstrelized, in between those two views is this evocative, poignant incursion into Africanistic space—but the book is unable to bear further entrance into that area because the narrative is Huck's—about Huck and his freedom. Also the first person point of view not only prevents us from entering Jim's interior life, but also protects us from ever seeing Jim alone, without Huck, thinking his own thoughts and perhaps contesting those he has been given.

2. CONFLICT BETWEEN ETHICS AND INSTITUTIONALIZED RELIGION

Frequently, no, more than that—virtually *every* instance of contemplation regarding the right thing to do (as well as his decision to enact moral choices) is connected to Jim.

pp. 8–9 Huck's loneliness/thoughts of death followed by p. 10 encounter with Jim at which Huck itches and Tom wants to tie Jim up for fun. Huck declines.

pp. 14–15 Huck's ethical confusion when Jim is not around.

p. 17 Huck, independent of Tom, recognizes "Sunday School" ethics. Tom is all protocol and capitalist gangsterism.

p. 56 moral balancing Huck and Jim do—comic but influential

p. 147 Huck tells truth *after* discovering Mary Jane's grief over the loss of her slave. This is apparently something Huck can identify with.

p. 166 condemnation of whites selling slaves, Huck says *we*

p. 167 Huck's ethically anchored (but religiously sinful) decision regarding whether or not to turn Jim in *cleans* him. When he destroys the letter he has taken the risk of "hell"; which in this context is the risk of maintaining moral stature.

3. MEANING OF FREEDOM

p. 38 and pp. 8–9 It seems that freedom without Jim is loneliness.
pp. 78–79 when Huck is separated from Jim, on land he
    sees white Americans fighting (not just "corrupt" shore—
    "innocent" river)
pp. 55, 95, 97 freedom with Jim is safe. [*READ*]

Freedom for Huck is not the white male rights of his father, that is, his life as an adult white male. But it is interesting to note that Pap's definition of white male rights exists only in relation to slaves. (p. 26)

Pap's is a dominating relationship—Huck's relationship with slaves alters its dependency.

Furthermore Jim's own freedom—a life without Huck—is clearly understood to be a threat—to Huck, to Tom, to Mark Twain's novel.

p. 73 Huck is made very nervous by Jim's talk of freedom
p. 77 the missing of Cairo and Jim's freedom. Seems false, the
    canoe is gone—fortuitously but inexplicably; and somehow
    for some strange reason Huck is too good to steal one.
    His excuse is that it would set people on their trail. But
    no one is looking for Huck; and they have stolen happily
    before.

Perhaps they miss Cairo (and don't even try for other Illinois landings) because the novel cannot survive without Jim; because the learning process, the evolution into a complicated complex person cannot go forward without Jim.

But most importantly, the very meaning of freedom is demonstrated in the baroque and problematic ending to which I referred earlier (p. 175). This elaborate deferment of Jim's freedom has been explained in several ways:

> I suggest that Mark Twain had a very definite plan in the final episode which depends on repetitions and variations of themes presented earlier in the novel. His primary objective in the "fatal" last chapters is to ridicule, in the manner of *Don Quixote,* the romantic tradition as exemplified by Tom Sawyer, who lacks character, who is full of purposeless fun; and to win final sympathy for the realistic tradition and its hero, Huck, who has achieved a sense of responsibility and a meaningful vision of life. In *Life on the Mississippi* (1883), Twain had already suggested his deep concern with the unwholesome effects of romanticism: "A curious exemplification of the power of a single book for good or harm is shown in the effects wrought by *Don Quixote* and those wrought by *Ivanhoe.* The first swept the world's admiration for the medieval chivalry silliness out of existence; and the other restored it. As far as our South is concerned, the good work done by Cervantes is pretty nearly a dead letter, so effectually has Scott's pernicious work undermined it." With *Huckleberry Finn,* Twain tries to "kill" romanticism. He suggests this obliquely by recording the fate of two ships prior to the last episode of the novel: the "Lally Rock" (a reference to Thomas Moore's romantic poem, "Lalla Rookh") blows up and the "Walter Scott" becomes a "wreck."
>
> There are other objectives in the last chapters. Besides ridiculing Tom's romantic vision, Twain neatly finishes off with other dominant themes dealt with in previous episodes: man's inhumanity to man, and Huck's faith in Jim's humanity.
>
> For with Ch. XXXIV, Huck is no longer the lieutenant who blindly submits to his leader's romantic schemes—which are not harmless ones now because Jim's life is at stake. For every exaggerated plan Tom proposes in the final episode (each one proves he is

sinning against Jim), Huck comes up with a practical one in such a way that the reader realizes that he is challenging Tom's previously unquestioned authority. This is evident when Tom plans Jim's escape. First, Tom says: "I wish there was a moat to this cabin. If we get time, the night of the escape, we'll dig one." Huck replies: "What do we want of a moat when we're going to snake him out from under the cabin?"

The controversy surrounding TS Eliot's and Lionel Trilling's claims for Twain's novel being an American masterpiece . . . this controversy was acted out in and around the ending.

Two things occur to me regarding this ending.

One, if this is truly an "American" novel of the nineteenth century, post-reconstruction, then one of its features, if not its major feature, is that there is no novel without Jim's presence; without this Africanist presence. When he is freed, the novel is over.

Two, the manner of the ending, its ornateness, its reduction from the adult plane on which Huck has been functioning to a less and lower one of not just boyish humor, but real degradation of their own imagination as well as the degradation of this man who has been their companion. Tom's chicanery for the sake of adventure; his insensitivity which Huck remarks upon is sustained and tedious. Some critics say that it returns Huck to the submissive role he has always assumed with Tom, just as it turns Jim into a plaything as he was in the beginning. In any case, it seems to me that the theatricality of the ending, which is after all ten chapters, almost a fifth of the book, *joins Tom and Huck,* merges the middle class and the poor class over the body of Jim—just as the Jim Crow and the minstrelsy performances did.

Twain's struggle with violence and stillness is profound in this novel. Contrasting with the magnificent stillness of the Mississippi River—the lyric, the nostalgic, the uninterventionist nature of these meditations—is the violence Pritchett was so alarmed by.

The peculiar power of American nostalgia is that it is not only harking back to something lost in the past, but suggests also the tragedy of a lost future. As Huck Finn and old Jim drift down the Mississippi from one horrifying little town to the next and hear the voices of men quietly swearing at one another across the water; as they pass the time of day with the scroungers, rogues, murderers, the lonely women, the frothing revivalists, the maundering boatmen and fantastic drunks of the river towns, we see the human wastage that is left in the wake of a great effort of the human will, the hopes frustrated, the idealism which has been whittled down to eccentricity and craft. These people are the price paid for building a new country.

For if this is a great comic book it is also a book of terror and brutality. Think of the scenes: Pap with d.t.'s chasing Huck round the cabin with a knife; Huck sitting up all night with a gun preparing to shoot the old man; Huck's early familiarity with corpses; the pig-killing scene; the sight of the frame house (evidently some sort of brothel) floating down the Mississippi with a murdered man in it; the fantastic events at the Southerner's house where two families are shooting each other down in a vendetta; the drunken Boggs who comes into town to pick a quarrel and is eventually coolly shot dead before the eyes of his screaming young daughter by the man he has insulted. The "Duke" and "the King," those cynical rascals whose adventures liven up the second half of the story, are sharpers, twisters, and crooks of the lowest kind. Yet a child is relating all this with a child's detachment and with a touch of morbidity. Marvelous as it all is as picaresque episode and as a description of the mess of frontier life, it is strong meat.

Gertrude Stein

I have read somewhere that there are two responses to chaos: naming and violence. The naming is accomplished effortlessly when there is a so-called unnamed, or stripped-of-names population or geography available for the process. Otherwise one has to be content with forcible re-naming. Violence is understood as an inevitable response to chaos—the untamed, the wild, the savage—as well as a beneficial one. When one conquers a land, the execution of the conquest, indeed its point, is to control it by re-shaping, moving, cutting it down or through. And that is understood to be the obligation of industrial and/or cultural progress. This latter encounter with chaos, unfortunately, is not limited to land, borders, natural resources. In order to effect the industrial progress it is also necessary to do violence to the people who inhabit the land—for they will resist and render themselves anarchic, *part* of the chaos, and in certain cases the control has included introducing new and destructive forms of hierarchy, when successful, and attempts at genocide when not.

There is a third response to chaos, which I have not read about, which is stillness. Stillness is what lies in awe, in meditation; stillness also lies in passivity and dumbfoundedness. It may be that the early Americans contemplated all three: naming, violence, and stillness. Certainly this latter surfaces (or seems to) in Emerson, Thoreau, and the observer quality of Hawthorne. It is traceable in the Puritan ethos as well. But unlike the indigenous population of America, and unlike the bulk of the populations brought to America from Africa, the American stillness was braced with, even mitigated by, pragmatism. There was always an aspect of preparing for heirs, a distant future unresponsive to the past, and the virtue of wealth as God's bounty—which it was a sin not to accumulate. This highly materialistic "stillness" as practiced by the clerical/religious immigrants was in marked contrast to the "take only what you need and leave the land as you found it" philosophy of pre-industrial societies. One of the more interesting matters in the Christian formation of public and private responsibility is the negotiation between thrift and awe; religious solace and natural exploitation; physical repression and spiritual bounty; the sacred and the profane. That negotiation persists in the tension among these three responses to chaos: naming, violence, and stillness. Although the majority of settlers in America were by no means the panicked religious or the kind but gloomy Plymouth Rock crowd of national reverence, convenient commodification, and nostalgic delusion. I believe some 16 percent were, but that leaves 84 percent "other" as they say on censorship forms. Yet even among that 16 percent it did not take long for that already ambivalent idea and complicity in stillness to dissipate in the wake of industrialization. With the abundant supply of free labor in the form of slaves, indentured servants, convicts, and term debtors, and of cheap labor in the form of poor immigrants fleeing from indebtedness, starvation, and death. Even as Twain privileged rural and village life, language and humor, even as he endowed the Mississippi and the lanes and roads of nineteenth-century America with pastoral yearning, he invested in profit-making schemes himself, disastrously as it turned out, and clearly urged and enjoyed the search for gold and the cleverness of money-making schemes in his characters. And it was our retiring, transcendentalist scholar Ralph Waldo Emerson who wrote of the California gold rush that "it did matter what immoral means were used: the function of the gold rush was to hasten the settlement and *civilizing* of the West." The underscoring of civilizing is mine.

Melville, of course, was preoccupied with the counter-claims of a blossoming capitalism as it mirrored or impaled itself upon the force of nature. And along with much else, *Moby-Dick, Billy Budd, White-Jacket,* and *Benito Cereno* address the impact of economic pressure on the "innocent" naif laborer and his "captain." All within the context of that two-thirds of the globe that represents chaos—the sea—and which seems to illustrate most clearly all three responses: naming (charting, mapping, describing), violence (conquest, whaling, slave ship, the naval fleet, etc.), and stillness (clams, soul searching, idle watches aboard ships that produce the most self-reflective passages in Melville). Poe it seems responded to chaos with violence and naming. Violence in his attraction to the damned, the dying, the murderer's mind. Naming in his insistent "scientific" footnotes, editorializing, indexing of historical and geographical data. But there was an additional element available to these writers, indeed to all Americans, for the contemplation of chaos. Nature, the "virgin" west, space, the proximity of death—all these mattered. Yet it was the availability of a domestic chaos, an invented disorder, a presumed uncivilized, savage, eternal, and timeless "other" that gives American history its peculiar and special formulation. This "other," as we have suggested, was the Africanistic presence. American colonialists and their heirs could and did respond to this serviceable, controllable "chaos" by naming, violence, and, very late in the day, tentatively, carefully, hesitantly, a measure of pragmatic stillness. Again it is to the literature, the writers, that we turn for evidence and figurations of this meditation on dominance. There one sees stillness (in Melville, for example) in the refusal to name in order to contemplate the mystery, the message of chaos's own inscription. In the refusal to do violence to, the refusal to conquer, to exploit. But to contemplate, to ruminate, to discover in this Presence a guide to the recesses of one's own mind.

It is in this context that I wish to discuss Gertrude Stein: her investigation of the interior life of the Other as a project of the investigation of the self; the problems that "stillness" or non-intervention presented and those same problems that her work fell victim to; when her exploration became exploitation and dominance; when her encounter with Africanism became awe, clarity, and wonder.

The "modernism" of which Stein is generally understood to be precursor has many forms: If we consider modernism to have as its single most consistent characteristic the merging of forms, the raveling away of borders, of frontier-lessness, the mixing of media, the blending of genres, the redefinition of gender, of traditional roles, the appropriation of various and formerly separate disciplines in the service of new or conventional ones, the combination of historical periods and styles in art—then we can trace the particular ways in which American literature made that journey. In America, the first mark and fearful sign of merging, of mixing and the dissolution of what were held to be "natural" borders, was racial merging. It was the best represented, most alarming, most legislated against, and most desired foray into forbidden, unknown, dangerous territory, for it represented the slide into darkness, the outlawed and illicit; the provocative, shocking break with the familiar.

In terms of literary embraces of modernism, as is also true of the visual arts' move toward modernism, the imaginative terrain upon which this journey took place was and is in a very large measure the presence of the racial "other." Explicit or implicit, this presence informs in significant, compelling, and inescapable ways the shape of American literature. Ready to hand for the literary imagination, it constituted both a visible and invisible mediating force. So that even, and especially, when American texts are not "about" Africanistic presences, the shadow hovers there, in implication, in sign, in line of demarcation. Several times in these lectures we have stressed that it is no accident and no mistake that immigrant populations understood their "Americanness" as an opposition to the resident black population—and still do.

For the intellectual and imaginative adventure of writers who have come to signify "modern" in literature, this convenient Africanist other was body, mind, chaos, kindness and love, the absence of restraint, the presence of restraint, the contemplation of freedom, the problem of aggression, the exploration of ethics and morality, the obligations of the social contract, the cross of religion, and the ramifications of power. The authors, American, who escape this influence are the ones who left the country—but not all of them.

Some astute critical observers believe that individualism American style precluded the possibility of, any room for, an "other" and that, in the case of sexism, it was an erasure of the other as significant, as a non-person. I wonder whether it is quite the contrary; that individualism emanates from the positioning of a safely bound self, out there. That there could be no inside, no stable, durable, individual self without the careful plotting and fabrication of an extrinsic gender, and likewise, an extrinsic, external shadow. Both are connected, but only at the outer limits of the self, the body.

(It has been pointed out to me that whenever the film industry wishes to and does manifest some brand-new technology or scope it employs Africanistic characters, narrative, or idiom. The first full-scale speaking film was *The Jazz Singer;* the first box-office hit was *Birth of a Nation*; the first situation comedy on television was *Amos and Andy,* and, although this does not quite fit, but it almost does, the first documentary was *Nanook of the North.* And there is probably no contest from any quarter that the informing scores of "modern" filmmakers have been what we call in the States "black music.")

Twice in these lectures we have suggested that the salient characteristics of American literature—its newness, its difference, its individualism, its tendency to feature a powerful and heroic common man—are characteristics dependent wholly or in part on an

Africanistic presence for definition. We are further suggesting that these terms altered with World War I: newness became innocence; difference for its own sake became the hallmark of the modern; individualism became alienation; and the heroic common man became anti-heroic, cynical, sullen, hard-bitten. Each of these terms, as well, seems to me informed by a complex awareness and employment of a constituted Africanism as the training ground and stadia for its contours. What are Americans innocent of if not an oppressive and parasitical relationship to that population that defined their whiteness? What is the relationship between the different, the "modern," to the actively creative presence of African-Americans? What is the individual alienated from if not his or her "white" self in an abiding but somehow fraudulently maintained and articulated pluralism? How does the cynical and hard-bitten common man achieve his status, if not in relation to racial hierarchy and sexual hierarchy? Hero or anti-hero, he must hold, withhold, or distribute power along lines of race and gender.

Virtually all of these matters surface in the work of Gertrude Stein. She is, of course, understood to be a paradigm or a precursor of modernism, so it is of especial interest to us to locate connections, if any, between her literary preoccupations, her innovations, what she makes of "difference," of individuality, of her perceptions of sexual power and the privileges emanating from class and race—and what we understand to be modern literature.

Gertrude Stein's remarks about her work are not always helpful when reading her for the first time, but I do recommend some examination of the collection of her lectures when she toured the United States. In that collection, entitled *Gertrude Stein Lectures in America,* there are two pieces relevant here: "The Making of the Making of Americans" and "Portraits and Repetition." In these two lectures, reprinted as essays, Miss Stein gives the genesis of her thinking about writing: its need for "repetition," the difference between "repetition" and "insistence"; how each person has a separate and vitally interesting story. Her announced project when she left medical school was to do the work without end—a book to be called *The Long Gay Book*. Paradoxically her view of the worthiness of each individual's narrative would result in the commonality of all of them—their emotional lives, so to speak, would persuade us that we are, in our differences and uniqueness, common. It is also in this lecture tour that she describes the difference between English literature and American literature, saying that the former did not have or need to use difference; while the latter—American literature—most certainly had to be and create difference. Now it's true that Stein has a way of making the obvious obscure, of making operas out of infantile observations, more often than not deep down in her language among all of that *simplicity* is a glowing coal of intelligence. In the matter of noting the absence of difference in one national literature and its vehement worked-up presence in another (American literature), I think she is on to something.

Her language, also, presents an opportunity to discover something about what may be called modern American prose. In the lectures she stresses her use of "new" English to say what "new" English is. I won't try to clarify her position here, except to say she was interested in the surgical, the revelation available to us in the unadorned; and the crucial importance of listening—thus her repetitions are not tedious, or if they are, they are so much so, the term becomes irrelevant as we find ourselves not just hearing but listening to a simple word and thereby becoming aware of its meaning in a profoundly new sense.

What she wished to accomplish by her repetitions and what she did in fact accomplish is a matter for some interesting speculation. Certainly there is a compelling music in her prose, and compared to the kind of descriptive language being written at the turn of the century [*Three Lives* was copyrighted in 1909] there is a world of difference. And I think we can safely say that *difference* was Miss Stein's persistent interest. She wanted to write a book that included everybody in it, and each narrative would be—"different." Her own style of living, while not entirely in a class by itself, could be called brilliantly out of the ordinary, and there was little in her own writing that could be called representative, imitative, or even related to the writing that preceded and accompanied her own. Indeed, so different was her language and her intentions for language that she may have become the writer other writers became different through.

Of the works she is remembered for best, there is no doubt *The Autobiography of Alice B. Toklas* is monumental—writing from the point of view of one's companion writing about oneself is still an amazing feat as well as a singular idea. What is more, she carried it off. In the narratives that make up *Three Lives* her yearning for delineating difference is further satisfied as she treats the lives of three women of a class, education, and background quite different from her own. What is interesting in this work is, on the one hand the distinguishing difference Stein makes among these women, and the differences she enforces, fabricates, employs, in the character whose life takes up by far the most space and is literally and figuratively the center of the piece. An occupying center so heavily worked out, the book would have no gravity at all without it. The three women do not represent merely differing narratives, or merely dissimilar kinds of characters. One of them, the central figure, is the differentiating principle that binds the other two. Melanctha is not only a different character among three, she is or becomes the strategy of differentiation itself and as such offers Stein opportunities for her prodigious imagination that even she seems not to have taken elsewhere in print. Melanctha becomes the available but forbidden territory that her difference makes safe to explore. She becomes the serviceable body/territory/ language available for explorations into forbidden topics—of carnal knowledge, of homoerotic love, of orations made intellectually safe by the protective coloring difference affords. Her color renders her different, and because of color she is there, one might say, for the taking.

The three lives Gertrude Stein renders in her novel of that name are decidedly unequal. Not only in treatment, as I hope to demonstrate, but also in various other ways. Of the three women that comprise this work (a work of three stories put together to make a novel or novella) one covers 71 pages, another requires 40 pages, and another, the central and middle narrative, takes up twice the length of one and almost four times the space of another. This unequal distribution of space, each of which focuses on one woman, is marked by a further differing inequality. The first part is called "The Good Anna"; the last part is called "The Gentle Lena." Only the central, centered, and longest part has no adjective; it is called "Melanctha." Simply. As you will remember, Melanctha is a black woman (or as Miss Stein identifies her, a Negro [?]). Sandwiched in between the two others, she appears framed, bounded by the others as though to foreground and underscore her difference while keeping it firmly under control. Before I get into the remarkable differences between Melanctha and the two women who stand to her right and to her left, I should perhaps identify the similarities—for there are some although they seem to throw further into relief Melanctha's difference, and the difference Stein makes of her. All three women comprising this text are servants; all die in the end; all are mistreated in some fashion by men or the consequences of male-dominated society. All are at the line between abject poverty and deserving poverty. And although all were born in some country, the similarities end precisely at this point. The two white women have a nationality: German, first, and then, as immigrants, they can assume the category German-American if they choose. Only Melanctha was born in the United States, and only Melanctha is given no national identification. She is a Negro, and therefore even in 1909, forty years after the proclamation freed all slaves, she is without a land, without a citizenship designation. She is never described as an American and certainly never labeled one by the narrator. Lena came to Bridgeport from Germany with the help of her cousin; Anna came to the States after some years of domestic service in south Germany, looking for similar, but presumably better paid, work. Both Lena and Anna are presumed to have had some process of Americanization—other than just showing up—that Melanctha can never have. What *Three Lives* seems to suggest is what that process is.

For Miss Stein, Melanctha is a special kind of Negro. An acceptable one for she has light skin, and the point has power when we note that her section opens with the comparison between Melanctha and her very close friend, Rose, who is described repeatedly (insistently) as very black, "sullen, childish, cowardly, black Rosie grumbled and fussed and howled and made herself to be an abomination and like a simple beast." [p. 85] Within this collection of adjectives are all of the fetishes, forms of metonymic reduction, collapse of persons into animals to foreclose dialogue and identification and economical stereotyping that is pervasive in the implications, if not the explicit language, of most pre-1980 fictional descriptions of Africanistic characters. "Rose Johnson was a real black, tall, well built, sullen, stupid, childlike, good looking negress." [p. 85] "Rose Johnson was a real black negress *but* [italics mine] she had been brought up quite like their own child by white folks." [p. 86] We note at once that it is not necessary for Stein to describe or identify these white folks, to say whether they were good, or well educated, or poor, or stupid or mean. It is enough apparently that they were white, the assumption being that whatever kind of white people they were, they were *that*, and therefore the instruction given to Rose would place her in a privileged position, a fact that Rose herself not only acknowledges but is grateful for. Melanctha, on the other hand, being light-skinned, is described as "patient, submissive, soothing, and untiring." [p. 85] She is also a "graceful, pale yellow, intelligent negress," who has "not been raised like Rose by white folks but then she had been *half made with real white blood* [italics mine]." The point is redundantly clear. While Rose can claim the good fortune of being reared by white people, Melanctha has the higher claim, the blood claim. There is some carelessness here, for we are later made to understand that Melanctha's father was "very black" and "brutal" and her mother was a "sweet appearing and dignified and pleasant pale yellow colored woman" [p. 90]. This does not suggest the "half white" label. Although Stein calls Melanctha a "subtle, intelligent, attractive half white girl," [p. 86] according to the racial genetics of the day, a half white person would have to have one white parent. I think this latter possibility would offer too much complexity for the author [she would have had to explain how the white parent (in this case the mother, since the father is pointedly black) happened to get together with the black parent], and it is perhaps sufficient that Melanctha's white lover is later on examined as pivotal to her destruction without having to go into the ramifications of another mixed-blood relationship.

I am not repeating these routine racial lapses and linguistic short-cuts aimlessly, but to stress the fact that the recourse Stein has to them, in order to draw certain conclusions, is so necessary either she is willing to make glaring errors in the finer points of racialism and to risk losing the reader's trust or she loses control of her wayward and insubordinate text. For example: Rose Johnson is repeatedly called childlike and immoral. But she is the only one of Melanctha's friends who sustains adult responsibility, a marriage, a house, some generosity. Stein asserts Rose's stupidity, but fails to dramatize it. We find no evidence whatsoever of her being stupid. And in spite of Melanctha's revered white blood, she spends most of her time in the streets, along the docks, and railroad yards. One has to question the logic of this blood fetish: perhaps it is her "white" blood rather than her black that encourages this immorality that Stein does not remark upon.

Equally interesting is the role of African-American men in Melanctha's story. That is, the place of fathers, husbands, friends of fathers as well as the beau in Melanctha's life. To Stein's credit, there is equal distribution of virtue and malice among the white and black men; to her discredit, she relies heavily on national stereotyping for them all: Irish prejudices, German ones, and, as is clear from the obsessive blood fetish mentioned earlier, conventional ones. Such pseudoscience ought to be surprising from one who attended medical school for a couple of years (the *New Orleans Medical Journal* article), but if Stein read medical journals she might have come upon the one just read. In any case, she abandons all responsibility to particularizing her Africanistic characters by "explaining" and "justifying" their behavior with the easy tools of metonymic reduction that skin color provides, and the economy of stereotype that is companion to it. Again, however, this strategy forces Stein into contradictions so profound, the trust of the reader dissipates altogether. For example, Melanctha's father is repeatedly described as "brutal and rough" to his daughter, and we are told that he is first a visitor to the household on an irregular basis, and then absents himself from them and the novel altogether. The evidence presented to us for his brutality and roughness is that he is "black and virile." When we look to see what this black, virile, brutal, and rough man is capable of, we see that: he protects his daughter from what he believed were advances made to her from a male friend and gets into a fight because of this protection. It is perhaps this contradiction that conveniently expels him from the text. Had he stayed, Melanctha would have had a fierce protector/ savior and not gotten into such deep trouble with men.

Most notably, however, are not the routine techniques of making the Africanist characters different *as blacks,* but what I believe is the reason for their inclusion in the first place, for the Melanctha section services Stein in a very specific way. The Africanism of that section becomes a means by which Stein can step safely into forbidden territory, articulate the illegal, the anarchic, ruminate upon the relations among women with and without men. Of all three of the women in the novel, only with Melanctha are sexual education and sexual relations central to the narrative and the fate of the characters. It may not have been thinkable, even for Gertrude Stein, to discuss, in 1909, explicit knowledge of carnal activities with white women—even if they were of a lower class. If we compare the sensuality/sexuality of Anna and Lena, we see that their lives are different from Melanctha's; they are chaste; their marriages arranged; their submission to the demands of patriarchy complete. It seems clear that, like other American writers, especially those we associate with modernism, Stein felt free to experiment with sexuality in narrative, felt the subject *palatable* if the object upon which these experiments are carried is Africanistic. Like the French doctor who was able to develop [the paradigm for] his gynecological instruments after sustained experiments with his black servant woman, Gertrude Stein is comfortable advancing her "newness," safe in her choice of forbidden territory because she is operating on a body that appears to be offered up to her without protest, without restraint. Wholly available for the articulation of the illegal, the illicit, the dangerous, the new. Like the white entertainers who were able to garner huge audiences when, in blackface, they spoke *through* the Africanistic persona, they could say the unspeakable, the forthrightly sexual, the subversively political.

What are some of these new and illicit topics?

There are at least three: (1) the intricate bonding of women not for protection but for the resources of knowledge they provide; (2) the triangular formation of sexuality, freedom, and knowledge as principal to a modern woman; and (3) the dependency of the construction of an American or an Africanistic Presence. There is a genuine even desperate love between Melanctha and Jane and Melanctha and Rose (in spite of the difference in their skin color). The sufferance and wisdom Melanctha receives from these friends is far superior to the things she learns from her men friends, from the black doctors, or black gamblers. All of the women in *Three Lives* come to a sad end, but it appears that only one, Melanctha, learns anything useful, and perhaps modern, about the world before her demise. It may be that in this respect, Stein's signal contribution to literature in her encounter with an Africanistic presence is to give this encounter the complexity and the modernity it had otherwise been denied by mainstream writers of that time. Although Stein's assumptions about white and black blood are traditionally racist, she provides an interesting variation on the theme by having Melanctha treasure the quality [if it can be called such] of blackness from her "unendurable" father; having the "very black" Rose advise Melanctha and persuade her not to commit suicide and be drawn as a "regularly" married woman with apparently very high standards of morality—denied by Stein's insistence that Rose "had the simple, promiscuous unmorality of the black people."

Key to Stein's exploration, however, is the question of the relationship of freedom for women to sexuality and knowledge. In this quest, we see again the difference she makes. *Three Lives* moves from the contemplation of an asexual spinster's life—the Good Anna—in its struggle for control and meaning, to and *through* the exploration of a quest for sexual knowledge [which Stein calls "wisdom"]—in the person and body of Melanctha, an Africanistic woman; to the presumably culminating female experience of marriage and birth—the Gentle Lena. That Stein chose a black woman for the examination of the erotic suggests and theatricalizes the uses of Africanism to represent and serve as license to address illicit sexuality.

Although Stein has her tongue in her own cheek for much of the text, has firm opinions that she puts in the mouths of others, and is forthrightly comic, even parodic in some passages, we are eager to follow her fairly radical look into the true lives of these women but in only one of them [Melanctha] does the sexual repression of the other two not only disappear, but its repudiation becomes the central theme of Melanctha's and Stein's enterprise. The black woman alone provides access to a meditation on sexual knowledge, and it is of utmost importance that the author calls Melanctha's flirtations, her wanderings alone down to the docks and railroad depots to look at men, her promiscuity—all this she calls an eagerness for wisdom. The "very black" Rose is labeled promiscuous, but the half-white Melanctha is searching for knowledge. This difference in labels for presumably identical behavior is distancing and functions as a covert manner of giving dignity to one kind of inquisitiveness and discrediting another simply by marking a difference in the color of the inquirer's skin. Further differences are notable when the comparison is between the white servants and the black women. Neither Anna nor Lena are curious about sex. Good Anna never entertains the possibility of marriage or a love. Her "romance" is with her first close friend, Mrs. L. Gentle Lena is so terrified, dull, and uninquisitive, Stein does not have to speculate on the legal sexual intercourse that takes place between Lena and her husband, Herman. She simply delivers four children, dying with the last and leaving her husband quiet, content, and himself a nurturer. Only Melanctha has courage, feels the attractive power of her black father, and the weakness of her pale yellow mother, senses that her identification with her passive mother will give her no respect; she is free to roam the streets, stand on corners, visit the scene of black men at work on the railroad, at the docks; to compete with them in fearlessness, trade with and trade barbs with them, tease and escape from them—and to talk back to them. This lingering over the "freedom" of an Africanistic woman is unique, I think, in American literature. It is Melanctha's authoritative voice that examines, articulates, and questions erotic heterosexual love; which combats the middle class's ideal of domestic/romantic union and which boldly enters the field of male-female encounters as a warrior—a militant. It is interesting to me that in her probe of the value of carnal knowledge, Stein looks not toward the very black Rose, the one she ascribes unmorality and promiscuity to, but to the half-white, college-educated Melanctha. It is as though, fearless as she was, Stein could not bear to investigate these very intimate matters on the body of a very black woman—the risk of such an imaginative association seems to have been too much for her. One feels her disdain of Rose, but her admiration of Jane's loose behavior, like Melanctha's, is ambivalent and rendered in clearly elevated and cynical language. Jane Harden is identified as a "roughened woman. She had power and she liked to use it, she had much white blood and that made her see clear . . . Her white blood was strong in her and she had grit and endurance and a vital courage." There is no mistaking Stein's codified values and opinions regarding race. She is identifying her own self with the white blood that makes for clarity and strength and vital courage; but is working its sexual expression out on the not-white blood that courses through these bodies in apparently two separate veins. The ludicrousness of these claims of what white blood is capable of in its generic transfer of power, intelligence, and so on is, of course, emphasized by the fact that in the same breath, if not paragraph, we witness the behavior of completely white people, people with all white blood who are passive, stupid, and so on. If we were going to succumb to the idiocy of scientific racialism, the logic of the opposite would be unspeakable: that in *Three Lives* it is the black blood that provides the "vital courage and endurance." There is tension and some readerly distrust of these hierarchies and claims, because of the contradictions that accompany them. Africanistic women, for example, are suffused with loose immorality, but Mrs. L., the friend and major force in Lena's tiny world, spends her professional life midwifing and likes especially to deliver girls in trouble; she even seems to be involved in abortions with her wicked doctor lover at one point. Why these white girls in trouble are not also guilty of amorality and looseness as are their dark sisters is part of the question these matters put. That series of episodes is glazed over by pointing to the generosity of Mrs. L. and her skill. There is no lingering over the unmorality of her patients; they are not assumed to have a "promiscuous nature" because of their skin color, or even, it seems, to have been seeking the wisdom of the world down at the docks.

Earlier I said that *Three Lives* seems to suggest very strongly the logic of American nationality—the process that Anna and Lena seem to have undertaken that is neither required of nor available to Melanctha. Like Hemingway's Cubans, she is excluded without explanation or even rhetorical gesture from national identity—her only identity is raced and gendered. And it is the former, her race, that seems to allow nationality to the alien, the foreigner who gets his or her distinction in asserting and developing whiteness as a precondition to Americanness.

When Mathilde, a minor character in the Good Anna section, visits Germany, her mother's birthplace, and becomes embarrassed by Anna's peasant manners, her remark is that her cousin is "no better than a nigger." Miss Stein, fascinated with her project "The Making of Americans," has indeed delivered up to us a model case in literature: (1) build barriers in language and body; (2) establish difference in blood, skin, and human emotions; (3) place them in opposition to immigrants, and voilà! the true American arises!

Sandwiched in between a pair of immigrants—her aggression and power contained by the palms of chaste but restraining white women—Melanctha is bold but discredited; free to explore but bound by her color and confined by the white women on her left and her right, her foreground and her background, her beginning and her end, who precede her and follow her, and we can see that the structure and its interior workings say what is meant. All of the ingredients that have an impact on Americanness are on display in these women: labor, class, relations with the old world, forging an un-European new culture, defining freedom, avoiding bondage, seeking opportunity and power, situating the uses of oppression. These considerations are inextractable from any deliberation on how Americans selected, chose, constructed a national identity. In the process of choosing, the unselected, the unchosen, the detritus is as significant as the cumulative, built American. Among the explorations vital to the definition, one of the strongest is the rumination of Africanistic character as a laboratory experiment for confronting emotional, historical, and moral problems as well as intellectual entanglements with the serious questions of power, privilege, freedom, and equity. Is it not just possible that the union, the coalescence of what America is and was made of is incomplete without the place of Africanism in the formulation of this so-called "new" people, and what implications

such a formulation had for the claims of democracy and egalitarian-
ism as far as women and blacks were concerned. Is not the contradiction inherent in these two warring propositions, white democracy
and black repression, also reflected in the literature so deeply that it
marks and distinguishes its very heart.

Just as these two immigrants are literally *joined* like Siamese twins
to Melanctha, so are Americans joined to and defined by this Africanistic Presence at its spine.

William Styron

Offers an especially rich opportunity to examine some of the major themes we have suggested to Africanist discourse in American literature.

1. the deployment of certain linguistic techniques and strategies to insure, identify, or contest racial hierarchy: [*the list of selected terms*]

2. the shaping of a national self as we described in the William Dunbar excerpt from Bailyn's book *Voyagers to the West*.

3. the minstrel paradigm employed to join conflicting classes, groups, and arguments which cement the construction of whiteness.

4. controlling interior and social chaos, disorder, and anarchy by means of naming, violence of naming.

5. One we have not mentioned is perhaps central to the balance of the course. Positing a modern self. This is a process unlike the construction of a national self, in that the modern writer collapses the national self and begins to experiment with a process of transgression, crossing cultural borders, racial borders—in an effort to imagine and

sometimes to merge with the Africanistic other. This literary miscegenation, this sort of mixed-media process is rampant in the mid-twentieth-century literature and intensifies as the century moves on and closes. [Remember Charles Bon never knew he was black till very late in his short life, but Faulkner always did know—it can be understood as Faulkner's entering a black ????, as can the character Joe Christmas in *Light in August.* This is an important point because Faulkner always said that it was not possible for a white man to enter or understand the mind of a black.] This merging which I am suggesting is a mark of modernism, we have seen in Gertrude Stein and Hemingway, will see in Faulkner and Bellow and most dramatically in Styron as we watch him use Africanistic Character and the Africanistic narrative [the black escape plot] and Africanistic idiom, all of which he needs to merge as completely as possible in his imagination with a black man.

The questions we wish to put are What is the risk of this merging, this crossing over? What is to be gained? Reassertion of whiteness/ Americanness? Expansion of whiteness? Or loss of whiteness? What we are interested in is how related the process of positioning and becoming modern is to Africanism.

Prior to a discussion of *The Confessions of Nat Turner,* it may be profitable to look at the first novel of this writer, *Lie Down in Darkness,* completed when the author was a very young man [in his twenties, probably] and published in 1951. The date of publication requires us to recall the forties—the kind of state of the world America was in then. Immediately post–World War II—a war fought for a number of reasons but which has been historicized as the "good war" because, unlike others, the racism with which this one was consumed found its most malign expression in the technically and bureaucratically efficient slaughter of millions and millions of "others"—in this case

Jews, regardless of their politics, religion—whatever—were the targets of this racism. This is not to say that racialism played no part in previous and subsequent wars, but it is to say that the monstrous modernity of the attempted genocide of World War II must have been on everybody's mind in the late forties. That like other historical periods [the Civil War, the Opium Wars, the Mexican War, etc.] the text was racism and the period had to find a race-neutral vocabulary for what was patently the case. So Mr. Styron not only grew up in a region, Virginia, that was institutionally and historically racist, but he participated in a war that garnered its "good" qualities from being the one where the enemy was clearly, publicly, and, in its military policy, enthusiastically racist. One suspects that Styron has always been especially sensitive to these kinds of mindless cataclysms [and his subsequent novel, *Sophie's Choice,* is testimony to his abiding concern with racial "otherness." He has brought his considerable gifts as a writer to that investigation]. In any case, the examination of his novels is not only an examination of a literary/artistic confrontation with the "other," it is an opportunity to witness the evolutionary development of such a confrontation.

The Confessions of Nat Turner could have been written, and I believe was written, with the knowledge that it would have black readers—many, many black readers. It did, but the point here is that it had, unlike Mr. Styron's first novel, a referent outside the text that included African-Americans. As we have seen elsewhere, that referent, that awareness of the "eye" of the "other" [or the absence of that "eye"], is significant in that it forces the text to become dialogic rather than monologic. When the discourse of the text includes the other it can reveal interesting differences from a text that excludes the presence of the "other" entirely. In short, the Master Narrative alters, though it may not disappear [in fact, the uproar blacks caused regarding *Nat Turner* seemed to be in large part the offense that was taken at witnessing the Master re-inventing another Master Narrative to be delivered by the slave]. Our reading of *Nat Turner* is aided considerably by some familiarity with Mr. Styron's first novel, *Lie Down in Darkness*. For in that work there is no referent to, no consciousness of, the possibility of a black readership, and there should not necessarily be such a consciousness. But the fact is that Styron's encounter with and use of an Africanistic presence in this first work yields a great deal to think about precisely because it is unselfconscious. Whatever literary uses there are would not be racially agenda-ridden—Styron is therefore free to be free with such a presence, and we can therefore see what such a presence means and does to his writing and his imagination. What follows are observations on the first novel that serve to illuminate the achievement of *Nat Turner*.

1. The Title. Taken from the preacher's phrase at Peyton's funeral and referring clearly to death, grave, sleep, etc. Can just as easily, for our purposes, refer to the "rest," the eternity, the surround of and in darkness, shadow, and a persistent black presence.

2. Opening dotted with scenic ruminations and views of several black people. In establishing place, region, Styron gives us the quality of the locale by identifying the conductor on page one as having a "guttural and negroid" "voice"—so one knows where one is. On the next page the reader is invited to look at a fellow passenger sleeping with his lips parted, and shortly thereafter, out of the window at an old black man, plowing, with his mouth agape, pink gums showing. The man with the lips parted is asleep; the working black man, although much farther away, can be seen to have pink gums [everybody does, but one can't always see them from at least five hundred yards]. Here one wonders what expression is that? Is the black man smiling, grimacing, yawning, screaming, drooling, singing? We don't know, are not told, and, in fact, it doesn't matter. The point is made, or rather implied: the black man's face is doing something

odd, grotesque, something curiously negroid, and it does not matter what the emotion is or what the gesture emanates from. It is the first of the lines of demarcation in the emotional and sensible lives between his black characters and his white ones. The hand gesture of the black man—is it a wave?—is described as "cataleptic." A mouth agape, pink gums exposed, dark brown hand cataleptic—the man is an idiot and is lucky he can follow his mule. In the very next paragraph, some blacks are imagined to exist in the trees ["And most likely . . . a couple of Negroes . . ."]. They are working too, sawing trees for lumber, and although we do not know how long they have been there, they are interestingly ignorant of the destination of a train that passes every day. Is it going to Richmond or Port Warwick? Wherever it is headed, the destination has only a sexual reference for them: a poontang town. The narrator has been told a sexual joke a few lines above by his seat mate [two college girls at the Hostel Astor], but he imagines, places, invents explicit sexual desire as the sum total of the dreamed-up young blacks in the woods. On the fourth page of the text, we are introduced to the characters—no longer anonymous whites and blacks, but named people. Consider the introductory sentence. "From the back seat there emerged Milton Loftis, followed by a woman named Dolly Bonner, and by an old Negro woman dressed in black silk and white lace collar and cuffs. Her name was Ella Swan." Consider, first, the implications of a sentence Styron did not write: "From the back seat there emerged Milton Loftis, followed by a woman named Dolly Bonner and a woman dressed in black silk and white lace collar and cuffs named Ella Swan." In this latter sentence, there would have been confusion in the reader's mind of his view of things. What confusion? He may have thought Ella Swan was white. Or

possibly that she had stature considering her dress, the lace
and all. Ella Swan is not only the last to emerge:
she is a servant, and she is old. But most significantly is
the exclusion, the separateness that is not limited to her
status as a servant but spreads to the placement of her proper
name. She is not named as one of a sequence. Her name
is given its own sentence. Perhaps to confer on her some
special dignity or some special, dramatized place the reader
is to look forward to in the narrative. Perhaps she will
play a significant role, emerge as a character to watch out
for or simply watch. She doesn't. The separate sentence is
separateness, marginalization, literary marginalization like
the compositional marginalization in the painting about
the Mexican War. Marginalization, however, with a peculiar
intimacy. It is this combination of intimacy and separation
that is announced, real and on display in the grammar of
every construction.

3. Love. Ella Swan's love for the dead girl, her grief, which is
presented to us as sincere, does not help her escape from
being described as a wizened monkey. Her wrinkles are not
like the wrinkles of Mrs. Loftis. That latter is sad, but not
bestialized. [*more ck*].

The reader is invited to meditate, with Helen, on the only pure
example of love displayed in all their lives and in all of the novel:
that of her demented daughter Maudie and a half-black half-Indian
magician, whom she calls Bennie. We should wonder why his worker
is not white, and since he is not, is that why he can't or doesn't speak.
He is eloquent in magic, seeing, understanding, but not in speech.
What are we to make of this separate, gleaming interlude described
to us as the single true love—though doomed—in all of their expe-
riences? Such love is possible only between the damaged, the inar-
ticulate, the unreasoning, the innocent, the unsullied, the simple? If

either had any sense they would not have had such an encounter so full of interchange, so profound? Is the deep feeling and profound knowing of these two an example of the promise, possibility of love, or its impossibility? Unusual as it is, it is not ridiculed, demonized, as is the love expressed and articulated by La Ruth. This is Ella Swan's daughter who comes to help on Sundays. She works for the Loftises long enough to be mentioned when the Loftis children are nine years old (Peyton), as well as when she (Peyton) is away at school. The most memorable aspect of La Ruth is her body. She is described as very very large and very very unattractive. She is so large the house fairly trembles under her feet. She is first introduced to us when she breaks Loftis's reverie on a Sunday, saying "Mawnin, Mistah Loftis." In the next line she "shuffles through the room with a mop." In the sentence after that she is described as "a huge, slovenly Negro with steel-rimmed spectacles and an air of constant affliction." Mr. Loftis returns her greeting and asks about her health ["How's your back?"]. Her response is to "[lumber] past, mumbling something about misery, toiling up the stairs with a sullen flat-footed sound, a great, aching hulk of a woman, moaning and groaning." With all of the explicit and figurative language, the cluster of modifiers suggesting gigantism, laziness, and suspect pain [she is not afflicted—she has an air of being so], a woman the sound of whose footsteps is "sullen," whose complaints are real, in a way, but not to be taken seriously because they are merely "moaning and groaning," and remain undecipherable mumbles about "misery"—with all of this rather excessive devotion to rendering her, we don't really know much about her. Has she been ill with her back? How old is she? She is female because of her name and because the author says she is Ella Swan's daughter. But she is first described as a "huge, slovenly Negro with . . ." She is curiously desexed in that phrase. It is as if one wrote "a huge, slovenly Hungarian," "a huge, slovenly Brit," "a huge, slovenly Spaniard," "a huge, slovenly Jew, Catholic, Arab, Russian, Egyptian . . ." The picture is clear: the reader will assume maleness, if anything, but certainly not femaleness. The other possibility was to call her a huge, slovenly Negress. That term had some repute at one time, probably as recently as the forties, but I suspect there is another reason for La Ruth's absence of gender here, her absence of femaleness in a storm of repulsive modifiers—now I am not suggesting that Styron should have made her pretty or sweet or slight. Not at all. It is his character and he can see her or recall her in any terms he chooses, and he chooses to describe all sorts of people, black and not black, in as vivid a language as necessary, and they are a varied crew that people his book. He is critical, skeptical, scrupulously honest in his depiction of them. The interesting point about La Ruth is why is she here, in this paragraph, with nothing to do [on the surface, anyway] and is not heard from again for almost ninety pages. We don't wonder a great deal about her as she passes; we have seen her, we know who she is in real life, as they say. Everybody knows a La Ruth. Right? But the question persists. Why is she here at this moment and not her mother, say, or a swan, even? The answer may be found in what precedes her entrance and what follows it. Loftis, in the preceding paragraph, before La Ruth enters, is reminiscing about his mistress, Dolly, before she became his mistress—when he was deeply aroused by her. Some cigarette burn, some exchange, some flirtation. In any case thoughts of illicit sex are rampant. Throughout this passage he uses the word "pale" to describe Dolly no less than six times, and in one of them she says in response to his question of why she is so pale that she can not bear the sun. After this we see a crescent of pale breast. A dog barks, and La Ruth enters, the distinct and unmistakable opposite of Dolly, to do nothing but pass through with a mop. Styron could have stayed with the dog, Rover, but La Ruth fits the bill better for the shadow that is creeping into the narration by dint of her presence: Dolly is more desirable followed by La Ruth; her paleness (even six times) is paler followed by La Ruth; her charm is more charming followed by the sullen La Ruth, and most important, her sexlessness heightens the sexiness, the erotic reverie Loftis is having. If we doubt it, we are reassured by the thought that comes to Loftis immediately after La Ruth "moans and groans" in her vague nameless misery, "Well, Dolly, he thought . . . Well Dolly . . ." He jumps up to telephone her. No lyricism about sky and birds and seascape will do here; no chirping and play of light to present his lust for Dolly. The sensuality is evoked by that heavy shuffle through the page by the sexless, but erotic-sex-inspiring, sloven, but working on Sunday, complaining La Ruth. On the heels of her groaning complaints is Loftis "settle[d] back restfully." His rest is delicious, perhaps, because a black woman with a mop on Sunday is lumbering through her work. His desire is sharper, and seen to be so, when reflected against and measured against the woman without gender. La Ruth is very necessary to get this thing going: she gives it heft; she gives it meaning, she is the shadow that makes light possible. But this is Styron's La Ruth—not La Ruth's La Ruth. Whatever he wished her to be like or look like, she serves an enabling function here. She makes it possible for Loftis to think about Dolly, to rest, to conjure up erotic reveries, and it is extremely significant, those six uses of pale. Difference is desperately needed here, so even vague common Dolly gains status and desire when the background is a certain kind of Africanistic presence looming at the margin of the stage.

The second interesting appearance of La Ruth should also be looked at. It is a strange scene in many ways. La Ruth is overcome with grief at the death of Peyton, relates it to the loss of her own children, her own faith in Daddy Faith, advises Helen to take her husband back, and goes on at great and greatly intolerable length—passionate, insistent, loud. The scene is comic and it is also tragic. Her sensibilities are extreme. She so forgets herself she actually touches Helen, who is dumbfounded by the touch of Negro hands, outraged by the assumption of intimacy, speech, emotional relationship, the impertinence of a servant, the inconsiderateness, etc., etc. Again we have to ask ourselves, what is this scene about? Helen, drugged from pills taken to help her sleep, is wakened by La Ruth's ugly black mask.

During the balance of the scene she is upset by her own coldness about the death of her daughter—her unnatural unfeelingness, and the despair brought on by the fact that she feels nothing. Unnatural and unsympathetic as this is, she survives the scene with a great deal of reader sympathy by her juxtaposition to the monstrous, comic, uncontrolled feeling of La Ruth. The flight from that [La Ruth's] to coolness [Helen's] is explicitly in the line that ends the scene.

unvisited [ck] in reference to the black presences.

The heaviest significance, however, is in the ending. When all is lost and over. The book ends with the revival baptism scene and contains only black people. The hesitant one—the one distracted from the baptism—is La Ruth. Because she seems to be the only one thinking of Peyton's death and the sadness of the whole Loftis family. What are we to make of this final scene? Is redemption to be found among these people only? Is this the author's need for some simple-minded optimism, expiation—what? Why is he closing with a religious scene that instead of being beautiful is made ludicrous? What is the language of its "seriousness" and its "not-to-be-taken-seriously"ness? It is indeed passing strange.

There is a further question: Whatever this book is about—compassion, understanding for some thoroughly unlikable, emotionally untrustworthy, and compacted white Southerners, from whom we witness one single act of decency [Peyton soothing La Ruth], the fact is that we do have compassion because 1. Styron has a wonderfully lyric power and 2. he places this rather dreadful collection of family members against dreadfully described but emotionally licensed and freely compassionate black people. From the black man who helps Loftis out of the gutter to the heavy dependence on La Ruth's affections, there seems no getting around the conviction that because the blacks are "other" the author is free to employ their stereotyped characters, their language, and their stories to help his characters and his themes along. What would the story be like if all the black people in it were cut from it? If all the servants were white? If the final scene were a white evangelistic revival? If a white fat cook strolled through the room while Loftis thought about Dolly, or if a white cook trailed hotdogs behind her at a wedding while he thought of incest or repressed it? Of the first two questions, O'Connor could pull it off beautifully. The last two seem to require a La Ruth for contrast and suggestion of sexual anarchy. Keep in mind that Styron is male.

William Faulkner

Reading William Faulkner forces us to confront an aspect of the American (as a white male) unstressed or dormant in most of the preceding novels we have been reading: that of the patriarch. The exploration of the white male as "father," as paterfamilias creating and ruling a house including the family within it, is essential to our understanding of the American "self." There is Poe, whose houses are tombs, Hawthorne, Henry James, Scott Fitzgerald in *Gatsby*, but by and large most male American novelists tend not to foreground houses as the piston driving the narrative motor. At the time Faulkner was writing, playwrights such as O'Neill were delving most deeply into patriarchal households. Certainly when engaging in Africanist discourse, a moveable platform or neutral space is more frequently chosen. Whaleships, Riviera hotels, fishing boats, rafts, the easily dominated open space of Africa, the confining thoroughly dominated space of a prison cell. The choice of neutral or moveable space may be simply a more fruitful locus in which to imagine contact with an Africanist presence—while traveling one meets and observes people not normally in one's orbit. It may also be a safer choice, since the encounter does not require or imply permanence, and since either white or black characters can easily be made to move on and out of the site and even on and out of the narrative unproblematically.

The women writers, of course, are women and can be understood either to have more interest in the houses they occupy, manage, or feel imprisoned in, or to be excluded from "great events" and adventure (as warriors, political figures, explorers, hoboes, etc.) and concentrate therefore on domestic stories to stimulate their imaginations. Thus the imaginative encounter with Africanist people for women writers frequently takes place in houses—some of which are ruled by women, some not. Stowe, McCullers, Cather, and, although her Melanctha is street-lifed, Stein's two other women in *Three Lives* are housebound. O'Connor seems to be the only exception in our list, as she is the exception in many other ways.

For the men, however, the forests, jungles, savannahs, seas, rivers preclude domesticity, reduce it and the family as distant, repressive, or non-existent.

In the nineteenth century the contemplation of white male as paterfamilias was the contemplation of the Victorian household and all of its attendant values. In the fifth and final volume of *A History of Private Life* there is a compact description of the aspirations of the nineteenth-century American family.

"The ideal of family life in the United States was not invented by government propagandists, media moguls, or Madison Avenue tycoons; it was a product of middle-class American aspirations. In the 19th century it represented a tranquil haven against a competitive, often corrupt, public arena. In the 20th century it has become the focus of hopes for the good life—for a secure and stable home providing happiness as well as protection in a rapidly changing world. . . .

"Victorianism—that set of social and cultural values that characterized the white middle class in England and the United States during most of the 19th century—dominated cultural values in America long after the Victorian era came to an end. . . . [But] as early as the 1820s and 1830s what came to be called Victorian values were widely articulated in a profusion of advice books, popular stories, journals, dime novels, sermons, and exhortations of various sorts. Men and women were taught to fulfill separate but virtually interdependent functions. . . . Young men learned in church, at home, and in the popular literature what was expected of American manhood. The key element was moral autonomy: control over one's instincts and independent pursuit of one's calling. The core of this code was economic self-mastery. Ideally a man would be his own property, and control his own means of production. A striving man was the perfect citizen for his ambition furthered, rather than hindered, the goal of national progress."

This model, urged and accomplished in the early 1830s (during the time [1833] when Thomas Sutpen got married to his *proper* wife), this Victorian replica as it was constructed in the United States, if it were to be constructed in the South would inevitably require and include race and the powerful presence of Africanist personae, discourse, and narrative.

Nowhere has this darkness, this presence been more carefully dissected, explored, and commented on as it has in the work of William Faulkner. When he conceives of it, in the 1930s, the Victorian family is surrendering some of its codes and values to another model—a modern, post–World War I model—and struggling then and even now to maintain the vestiges of the pure Victorian family. Just as the Victorian period was made possible by the work and the wealth of African and Africanist people, their dominations, and their slaughter in the Golden Age of racism—so is Thomas Sutpen's Victorian house and family dependent on that same system of exploitation and peonage. Sutpen's project is to reproduce and maintain a Southernized Victorian household, to use and hold at bay the Africans and their descendants who are responsible for its construction, and to conceive of that house as a protection against disorder, and as the symbol of his status and his immortality.

Faulkner's imaginative approach to *Absalom, Absalom!* begins with an image that he kept repeating and discarding, repeating and discarding. It is the image of the Dark House.

In July 1931 Faulkner mailed to an editor a ms. entitled "Evangeline." There is no character called Evangeline in the story, but there is an Evangeline-like character in it—the one from Longfellow's poem of that title which features a pair of star-crossed lovers, and it is the name of a character in the story he wrote immediately following this one. Faulkner's "Evangeline" is organized as a dialogue between two men: an architect visiting the South to paint houses—mansions, Negro cabins and heads—and a first-person narrator: an "I." Here we see the beginnings of *Absalom, Absalom!* with its pair of men developing a narrative as they create it. The characters in this told story are Judith, Charles Bon, Sutpen, and an "old nigger great grandmother named Sutpen too," her granddaughter, and a dying Henry Sutpen. The plot revolves around bigamy, incest, and Bon's marriage to an Africanist woman—which (her "blood") is understood to be the primary and criminal act which destroys the lovers' union. In this story, Charles is white, but has *married* a black woman.

A few weeks later, in August of 1931, Faulkner began work on a project he entitled "The Dark House." He typed this title neatly on the ms. paper he liked to use: with a line at the top and along the right margin, and began the story of Jane Bundren, a pregnant woman walking twelve [?] miles to find the father of the baby she is carrying. One of the characters who befriends her and who becomes a major figure in the tale is a man named Joe Christmas. Joe Christmas thinks, says, wonders if he is black, and suffers the treatment meted out to blacks, although unlike the Charles Bon character in "Evangeline," but close to the Charles Bon to come, Joe Christmas is black without its markers. He looks white, but behaves black, admits black, works and lives as blacks do. There are no signs that are conclusive and we never learn if in fact he really *is* black. He presents, therefore, the most sinister aspect of racial hierarchy—it (blackness) can exist invisible to the eye, and can curse and pollute whether its biological signs are in place or not.

One of Faulkner's biographers, Frederick Karl, describes this novel as "basically a novel which remains out of the light—indeed a dark house, as the original manuscript title indicated." "The story is one of lights, darks, and twilights. It has to do with 'dark houses' and houses which are less dark, even to those which are light." He does not push the figure, however, beyond its superficial referents. According to Joseph Blotner, one of Faulkner's biographers, Faulkner sat in silence on his porch with his wife, Estelle, one afternoon, and she remarked on the quality of the light during that particular month—August. At which point her husband said, "That's it," and left her there on the porch to go into his study and cross out the neatly typed title, "The Dark House," and change it to *Light in August*.

Two years later (1933) Faulkner wrote a story about a man called Wash Jones, a "lower class" drinking partner of Sutpen's whose daughter is pregnant with Sutpen's baby. When the baby is born, Sutpen violates in a particularly insulting way Wash's own patriarchal yearnings—his family, his patrimony, his issue, his status, and his authority as a father figure.

Frederick Karl says the story "Wash" is "about the murder of a patriarch," that it is the tale of a king or emperor being brought down by his vassal. But Wash is not just a vassal, he is also a patriarch of sorts, an aspiring one, and the murders and suicide he commits are occasioned by both patriarchs' mis-reading of each other. Murder occurs at the very moment when the unifying properties of African-ism disappear.

Twice in this story Wash is ridiculed by blacks, and at the moment of the insult which leads to murder, Sutpen is discussing something he regards as more important than Milly's baby girl: that is the successful foaling of a horse—not a mare. And he is discussing this satisfaction over the body of the white girl with a black woman. The blow is devastating to Wash. Not just the indifference to his granddaughter, the privileging of the birth of a male animal over his own issue (and, not incidentally, the prioritizing of the black midwife's participatory conversation about it), but especially the crash of his ideal—his dream of joining perhaps but certainly being unified and associated with the planter class. The notion of the merging of that class with poor whites—is available through his delusions about his rank vis-à-vis black people. It is being treated literally "like a nigger," in his own house regarding his own issue that sends Wash into a rage neither he nor Sutpen and neither his daughter nor her baby will survive.

[*READ pp. 170 & ff. "Portable"*]

In March of that same year (1933) Faulkner began a series of starts on a book he knew or said he knew was the best book in America. Its working title was "The Dark House," and when finished in 1936, it included as its final scene the "Wash" material. Once again that phrase was erased and discarded for another, better one: *Absalom, Absalom!*

While each of these title alterations seems to me a marked improvement over "The Dark House," it is nevertheless fascinating to associate this continuously deleted working title for two projects, maybe three, with the image that must have been on Faulkner's mind. It is also interesting to contemplate Faulkner's own erasure of "darkness" and his repeated return to it as the mirroring act of the main theme in the novel under review.

In the first instance, "The Dark House" is erased for "Light in August," in which the problems of a dark racial identity and its mystifying presence (mystifying because unmarked and invisible) drive the narrative. The inability of anyone to actually "tell," the uncertainty in the narrative, the ambivalence the author himself has about whether indeed Joe Christmas is a Negro, all become irrelevant when the response to an Africanist persona is all that is necessary, to Joe and other characters, for the tragedy to ensue.

In the second instance of erasure, in *Absalom, Absalom!,* "Wash" is the final antagonist and the grounds for his murder of Sutpen are domestic matters, household matters—bloody solutions to the problems of patriarchy, and class hierarchy based on race, and tragic solutions to the problems of the white male American in his relationship to his house and his family.

"Evangeline," "Wash," and both of the "Dark House" narratives merge in *Absalom, Absalom!:* the "Wash" story becomes that novel's denouement, its full narrative being what precedes the murder and who was the man Wash murdered. It also concerns itself with major characters from "Evangeline"—one of whose presence in the novel is regarded as the source of the destruction and who, like Joe Christmas, figures a question without its accompanying question mark: the mark of race. Both Christmas and Bon carry darkness like a cross or a curse, although no one can see the darkness that damns them. Charles in "Evangeline" is white. Charles in *Absalom, Absalom!* may be.

What is or might be Faulkner's image of "the Dark House"? Karl describes it as though it were Rosa Coldfield's house, shuttered with Quentin Compson sitting in the dim and shadowy rooms. The "Wash" story suggests it was Sutpen's decaying mansion.

All of these images seem legitimate, and all illuminate some idea in Faulkner's imagination about a house or entity that is dark as in secret or dark as in sullied or dark as in menaced by what is the single most obvious factor in all of these stories: race, specifically the black race. The Africanist persona writ large.

What we have in *Absalom, Absalom!* is the consequence and effect of Africanism on the master's house.

Faulkner is singular among the male writers we have read in this course in looking closely at the American male not as lone traveler, unmarried or distant from his family; not as a temporary and transitional inhabitant of a beach house, hotel; but as the builder of a house and the placement within it of a family. Whatever else he is dreaming, Thomas Sutpen is dreaming himself up as a family man. [*READ p. 329 . . . "You see, I had a design in my mind . . ."*]

In 1831, the beginning of the time period of *Absalom, Absalom!*, the Victorian family was the English and American ideal. It was understood to be a fortress against disorder and anarchy. In England that disorder was the poor—the enemy within. In the United States it was a race of non-white peoples within. The Victorian house needed and lauded genealogical control as protection against two major threats to its solidity: women and blacks. Women are threatening to this house because unpoliced they let blacks in. Just as they intervene into Sutpen's project, disturb his design, spoil it, and make it vulnerable to disorder. [*READ p. 330 . . . "Conscience? Conscience? . . ."*]

Women are possessed by men, and obsessed by them. Like blacks, women have no existence other than their market exchange, the merchandise of "respectability," labor, sexual gratification, fecundity. And the serviceability between race and gender is mutual. The place of gender in the mythology of the Victorian house is a central repression in disguise. The "pure white woman" *holds back blackness; in one generation she could, if she wished, flood the population with black blood and render both blackness and whiteness indistinguishable,* thereby rendering the complete set of social and economic assumptions sundered. That is the heart of the terror; the feared and unacceptable thing to Henry Sutpen is not that the man his sister wishes to marry is already married—bigamy is awkward but manageable, nor is it the fact that the suitor is his and her half brother—incest is problematic but also not unmanageable in his moral code. The unacceptable thing is that his half brother Charles Bon has a trace of black blood.

In the Victorian house patriarchy is genealogy.

Genealogy is another word for blood, its purity and its genetic tracing. Genealogy is also the heart of male bonding: father and son, and the sons of the son. Genealogy is also power, authority, immortality, and private individuality.

So if in Faulkner's imagination the patriarch's house is *dark,* it is a signal for alarm. The modifier alerts us to this absence of light as an alteration, a disfigurement—something gone awry, turning the house away from its purpose—the maintenance of control against disorder and chance; turning it instead to that which is sinister, disorderly, destined, and corrupt. It is a darkness that disturbs genealogy, disrupts its planned progression by distorting, deferring, and repeating it in unacceptable ways. The house designed for unity is disunified by the same darkness that hides its internal divisions. The darkness of the house threatens to jump the barriers between the public and the private, and render helpless the walls of the fortress against the values imposed by the public. Thus the goal of privacy becomes the urgent need for secrecy. Darkness then is both fear of disorder and a necessary strategy; a rejection and a requirement.

Figuring out why Henry killed Charles Bon is the detective work that Shreve and Quentin pursue, and the puzzle is worked out by the detection that locates this Africanist presence. The consequences to the narrative and to Quentin are implosive. Quentin cannot be both inside and outside, observer and participant; he cannot know and deny that he knows. The effort to be and do both unhinges him. Although Quentin's problem (finding Africa) is *like* ours, it is *not* ours. Quentin's work is to locate an Africanist presence; Faulkner's project is to complicate both the process of locating it and the refusal to acknowledge it.

Faulkner problematizes the search for blackness in three ways:

First, he deconstructs race. The Africanist persona is not simply the signifiers that have formed it.

Second, race is merged with patriarchy. Union with the patriarch is deferred and delayed by race, and the mystery of the patriarch is cloaked by race.

Third, the language and structure of the novel both replicate racism and critique it.

The deconstruction of "race."

"Race" is defined as and recognized to be a *physical* difference, the most salient difference being color; secondary differences are hair, features, and something loosely described as "behavior." If these are the differences that matter, what happens to the definition when not one of them is evident? Race becomes what it in fact is: a socially constructed difference rather than a "natural" one serving purposes that are neither "natural" nor socially healthy or cohesive. Where race is easily and readily seen and spoken of is the very moment when it is most harmless and most ego-gratifying for "whiteness." Rosa's "wild niggers," the Negroes, boys and men, who carry messages from Rosa to Quentin, from Charles to Judith, midwives, servants who carry the tale, reveal the news, etc. Where race is not seen, where it is most invisible, most elusive, is exactly where it is most potent and most threatening.

If race cannot be *seen*, Faulkner shows us, then it must be something else, something other than its markers. This "other-than-its-markers" is what the novel requires us to search for, to contemplate. If race is hidden, and we are forced to *find* it, then we learn not much about race, but a great deal about racist discourse. Faulkner serves up to us this racist discourse in all its futility, madness, incoherence, and obsessiveness. Thus it is not race, but the discourse of race that menaces, ruins, paralyzes, corrupts, and annihilates. And paradoxically, it is the *discourse* that both represses and searches out race. Formulated in speech, memories, recapitulations, letters, dialogue, and monologues, the discourse of race, its narrative practices, the *idea* of race, and the construction of whiteness are exposed as sources of national tragedy.

The merging of race with patriarchy.

The patriarch in this Southern version, which is also the American version, is assertively, aggressively white. But to be white requires a close association with black. The merging of race and patriarchy is replete in the novel, as characters search for, cling to, and repudiate the "father" as they work to fathom his mystery and his meaning. Figurations blend the father's house with darkness, the father's law with racial supremacy.

The opening scene takes place in a dim room called "office" because the patriarch father called it that. We don't know what it would have been called by a wife or daughter who was not obedient. This daughter, Rosa Coldfield, agrees to and abides by the father designation, although the father has been dead almost forty years. "The blinds all closed and fastened for forty-three summers because . . . 'someone' . . . had believed light and breeze carried heat and that darkness was cooler." We are not told who the "someone" was, but it hardly matters because Rosa is the ideal citizen: law-abiding, law-loving, law-needing. Which is to say she is a child, as Faulkner makes clear immediately. She is sixty years old when we meet her, sitting in a too-large chair; her feet, incapable of reaching the floor, have an "air of impotent and static rage like children's feet." Furthermore, she is "embattled in virginity," the stage of female life, Faulkner implies, *prior* to her becoming a woman, an adult. Being therefore, a sixty-year-old law-abiding, father-needing virgin, she is "like a crucified child," living in her dead father's house which she has not thought or dared to alter, and which is described appropriately as "dim-coffin-smelling gloom, sweet and over sweet." The figures signify darkness, death, and a more than sweet ambience, but "over sweet," an embarrassingly sentimental one.

The ghost about whom Rosa is speaking, the patriarch, is said to be haunting Rosa's voice where a more fortunate ghost father "would have had a house [to haunt]." This ghost father is dispossessed of his own house and Rosa, dressed in black, becomes the dark house he is reduced to haunting.

When this ghost father was alive, when Rosa first describes him to us, she does so in terms that stress and freeze him as a disrupting race-framed figure engaged in house building. He and his blacks disrupt a peaceful, decorous, and, by strong implication, childishly innocent scene—"like a school-prize water color," Quentin imagines (and he bursts), into our imagination with the appropriated tools of the white American patriarch. He has appropriated Africa's wealth, labor, and power along with Europe's (in this case France's) ideals of civilization: art, aesthetics, "history" by association, and skill. In Rosa's language these representations of the "equipment" of patriarchy are called "wild niggers," half-tamed beasts, and white European history and aesthetics are chained like a slave to the patriarch. But representations, single-minded, repetitious, and impacted, are Faulkner's way of preventing us from surrendering to her version of Sutpen, as Quentin does. Quentin is young, impressionable, and overwhelmed by Rosa's insistent repetitive narrative. Thus he advances her image of the father. They both see the house he builds as quickly, almost immediately done, recalling the Godhead giving the first commands: "Let there be house. Let there be light. Let there be Sutpen's Hundred." In fact the building took five years, in fact it was not "dragged violently." It came about slowly, carefully, with abundant aid from Sutpen's workers, some of the townspeople and his own race-tainted cash. That she is unreliable is further stressed by her explanation of why she has to tell this story at all to Quentin—that he may wish to write it down someday, choosing as so many do a literary career. Quentin instantly thinks: "She don't mean that . . . It's because she wants it told."

Rosa's narrative is the first one to collapse race and patriarchy; the meaning of Sutpen's patriarchy is unavailable to her because it is cloaked in race—a cloaking she never recognizes or confronts. Because of her single-minded and impacted vision and narrative she never knows that racial darkness infuses the father's house, has penetrated the family members and seeps into every crevice, joint, and hinge of the house. She sees only the overt darkness of the black slaves who enabled the house, but not the covert, secret, and invisible racial darkness that destroys the father's house and all his issue. She relies on stereotype, depends on and reinforces racial hierarchy. And therefore she remains ignorant, unreliable, and "crucified." We come to understand this strategy as Faulkner's technique of commenting on and critiquing not the stereotype but those who do the stereotyping; not the content or subject of their narrative, but the narrative practices they engage in.

Further merging of race and patriarchy is inherent in the narrative: Charles Bon is held away from and rejected by his father because of race; Henry refuses to inherit the house or reproduce its line because of race; he also feels obligated to kill the brother who wishes to continue the line because of race; the patriarch Sutpen wants to be one because of the benefits of racial hierarchy which he discovers when he is refused entrance into a powerful white man's house by a black man; the "flaw" in his design is race; and he is murdered when the cloaking device of race disappears and he is left alone with the class problems between whites that he started out to obfuscate.

The language and structure of the novel replicate and critique racist strategies.

The purpose of racist strategy is to dominate and repress blackness. In order to do that, it has to locate blackness in order to purge, excise, and destroy it. We are treated, in *Absalom, Absalom!,* to the linguistic and structural display of the act of locating and repressing blackness. While the characters refuse to acknowledge, know, or confront the Africanist presence that informs and determines their every thought and activity, their past, present, and future, Faulkner forces the reader (through Shreve's persistence) to hunt for the Africanist presence, to trace it, to long to expose it. Faulkner renders our eagerness to find it desperate because we—like the characters—do not know where it is; not only because it is being kept away and out of sight, but also because it really is invisible. Being a social construct rather than a biological one. It is intrinsic, in the text and in the culture the text describes, yet, precisely because it resides on visible signs (color, etc.) neither the characters nor the reader can quite locate it. And although we are led to believe that race makes all the difference, we have to wonder why and how it matters if the difference it makes is no signed difference at all. The novel theatricalizes and comments on the process of repressing blackness by itself repressing it, and leading us straight toward it. The whole enterprise is to reveal the impact of this denial of blackness on the house of the patriarch.

Let us look at some instances where Faulkner forces the search *and* the revelation, and the strategies he employs to accomplish both: deferment, erasure, omissions, red herrings, hints, symbolic and metaphorical associations.

Rosa describes Sutpen's slaves on pp. 4–5 as a band of "wild niggers." On p. 41 the *author* identifies them again as "the bearded white man and the *twenty black ones,* and all stark naked beneath the croaching and pervading mud." We are led to believe the bank consists of twenty naked black men; but on p. 73, when Clytie's "mother" needs to be explained, we learn that there were two women among them—two black women slaves among the "band."

Also before we learn that Sutpen has a black daughter there is a previous unexplicit hint forty pages back when Rosa describes her sister Ellen's—that is Sutpen's wife—seeing the children in the loft. "But I was not there, I was not there to see the *two Sutpen faces this time*—once on Judith and once on the negro girl beside her." [p. 33] The "negro girl beside her" is an almost casual remark, and we may not at once absorb the preceding phrase, *two Sutpen faces.* That is to say, the negro girl is or has a Sutpen face. Now Rosa knows who this girl is, what her name is, her relationship to the Sutpens—everything. But we don't learn her name or that she is Sutpen's daughter until later [p. 73] and it is at that point that we discover the black women among the slaves he purchased. And it is also at that point that the first hint of another black child (other than Clytie) is made. The subtle, almost invisible reference to this child is couched in the passage about Sutpen's *naming* all of his children. "Yes. He named Clytie as he named them all, *the one before Clytie and Henry and Judith even . . .*" Who is "the one before"? On the same page that we learn what has been omitted earlier: that there were black women among his "band,"

and where we learn what has been withheld and deferred: that Clytemnestra or Clytie is also Sutpen's daughter by a black woman, we also are given the first of several hints in a long sequence of deferred information about Charles Bon: first that Sutpen has a son other than Henry; that this son is black; that aside from Sutpen, nobody knows this at all, including the black son himself, and of course William Faulkner. This black son's black mother is referred to before her son is as "that error" by Mr. Compson.

She is hidden in Mr. Coldfield's "unease" and "that old business." [*p. 77 READ*]

Then there are omissions that prove dangerous. For example, Rosa omits Clytie from the Sutpen's lineage on p. 167 and it is Clytie a few pages later who by her assertive presence as well as her hand paralyzes Rosa, prevents her climbing the stairs (until Judith intervenes). [*READ pp. 167, 170 & 171*]

But the most fatal erasure, the one that blossoms into the pivotal repression and the final denial, is in the narrative attempts to "absent" Charles Bon's blackness. It is a blackness buried and slowly disinterred. From the first buried trace of mention, an initial almost dismissed reference to him on p. 73—a reference in which we assume he is white because race does not figure at all in this first reference ("the one before"), we can chart the drawn-out disinterment of race, and the linguistic manipulations that direct our attention to a blackness that both eludes us and bursts from the seams. What the narrators try to join and explain, Charles Bon disrupts; what they try to repress, oozes; what they try to erase, explodes; what mythologies they try to reconstruct break down.

> P. 73—the first reference to Charles. Name and race
> unmentioned. But relationship *is*.
> P. 84. The second mention of Charles again withholds his race,
> but not his name "after [Henry] had brought Charles Bon
> home with him."

P. 85—the mystery of Charles is hinted at. Sutpen goes to New Orleans at the same time Charles returns there.

P. 87—a further hint with the phrase "nigger in the woodpile." (townspeople)

P. 90. This foreshadowing is further strengthened by metaphorical associations between Charles and Africanist figurations: he is described as being without childhood, timeless, "phoenix-like, full sprung from no childhood, born of no woman and impervious to time." But this foreshadowing is impaled on the cautionary phrase "must have appeared."

P. 91. The foreboding is subverted and deferred by Rosa's description of Charles as the garment, the furniture, and the tutoring "manners" of civilization. But that view is itself subverted by being called "the bright glitter of delusion."

P. 92. Deception and irony co-exist in the comment that "they [the Sutpen family] *deserve*" Charles.

P. 96. Further hints in the author's comment that the trouble that Christmas between Sutpen and Henry "came through the Negroes."

P. 110. We are led into part 1 of a false chase, a red herring. The secret seems to be that of Charles's wife—she is not racially pure. The question of what is the nature of Charles's unsuitability as Judith's husband has progressed as (1) he is a bigamist; (2) he has married a black woman; and (3) he will not renounce her.

P. 114. The false chase is given credibility as the real chase when Charles himself *reacts* like a white man, wondering why marriage to a black woman (which is illegal and easily aborted) would prevent his marriage to a white woman.

P. 123. We learn, by indirection, that the real reason for this unsuitability may not be Bon's black wife. [*READ*] The word *apparently* is introduced to give us pause.

Pp. 131, 132, 133—contain repetitions of withholdings, information held back and repressed. The phrase "what Sutpen told him" (that is, what Sutpen told Quentin's grandfather) is repeated several times, but the repetition serves to bind the secret, not expose it.

Pp. 109–160. The letter Charles writes to Judith proposing marriage confirms that he does not know he is black. The letter is held back from us and Quentin for fifty pages, heightening our interest in it. But when we read it, we learn nothing from Charles about the objections to his marriage. Almost nothing, that is, because the letter does go on and on about being written in stove polish. The very script he writes is not with the normal black of ink, but the strange, and excessively available, stolen black of stove polish.

This narrative sleight of hand, these stutterings, flashes of cards held up the author's sleeve, the literary foreplay, the slammed doors after peeps inside—duplicate the surreptitious, desperately urgent activity of hide-and-seek played with race. Hiding it and seeking it. As a game it energizes us, it wearies us; it enlivens us, it exhausts us; it provokes us; it stuns us—precisely as the burden of maintaining racist hierarchy does.

Reading Faulkner, as you must have guessed, is a major, and for some, a lifelong project. There is an almost limitless vein of riches in his work. I want to try now to use a few examples of the approaches to our study of American Africanism to this novel, hoping to clarify the enterprise and suggest how this writer fits into that study.

First we should look at the uses to which he puts the code language of Africanist discourse.

The literary dilemma of encountering Africanism is that the dilemma can prevent a writer any real identification with his society as a whole. The writer can be overwhelmed by the dilemma, retreat into its polarities, forswear the risk it poses to his or her imagination.

Such a writer is bound, then, to his or her race, identifying only with his or her color and, therefore, bound to distortion. Nadine Gordimer has said that "cultural identity [that is, identity with the whole of one's culture] is the ground on which the exploration of the self in the imaginative writer's hands makes a national literature."

What is most astonishing in William Faulkner is how he manipulates the code language of Africanist discourse, its strategies of mystification and oppression, in order to explore the paradoxes in the impact of an Africanist presence on the culture of the United States. He analyzes not the stereotype, but the characters who hold stereotypical views, and through his genius we see that there is nothing at all economical about stereotyping—it is, in human terms, as well as imaginative ones, extraordinarily wasteful. (For example, what a waste it would be to stereotype Sam Fathers in "The Bear." Faulkner takes him out of the society, the town, to describe what the wastefulness would be, and what it is when he returns him to the racist town.) Faulkner tracks the implications of metonymic displacement and the reliance on the fetishes it imposes. The devastating consequences of faith in "black blood" and "white blood." Thomas Sutpen could have avoided his and generations of grief had he acknowledged, even ignored following the acknowledgment, his son; or kept his first wife. Faulkner posits then interrupts metaphysical condensation by forcing characters to assume the obligations, the actions necessitated by that condensation or face irrelevancy. Ike McCaslin cannot rest, following the bear hunt when he reads the ledger kept by his grandfather and granduncle, until he makes the sustained attempt to right the wrong they set in motion. Quentin Compson's personal survival depends on his ability to know what such reductions have withheld and to take responsibility for them. His intellectual inaction dooms him. Faulkner's allegorical mechanisms disclose rather than foreclose the biblical allegories of the third and favorite son of David, called Absalom, who killed his half brother, Ammon, for having raped their sister Tamar; the Greek allegorical formulations of Agamemnon's fate and the fate of his line—Judith and Henry being a sort of Electra and Orestes, Clytie being more Cassandra—which Sutpen meant to name her, but said Clytemnestra instead, which would make this daughter a kind of wife to Sutpen, which she may well be since she cares for his house and his children and grandchildren and waits while he is away at war—these allegories disclose their fissures and break down in close encounters with Africanism. Clytie does not leave Sutpen's Hundred, nor desert with other blacks during the War not because she is a slave—there is no suggestion that she is or is treated like one by Judith or Sutpen; nor because she expects to inherit the estate. She stays because Judith is her sister; and she stays on after Judith dies because Henry is her brother, just as Charles Bon is. If you follow that Greek allegory of Clytemnestra through—with Clytie being Charles's sister (as well as Sutpen's "wife") you get an incestuous entanglement that hardly bears thinking about.

The text is written in disjointed, evasive repetitious language which Faulkner deploys not to escape history, but to force us to put it back together. To join, specify, and make meaningful. Which is to say, that when the work is done and history is put back together, studied, made coherent by our filling in the gaps, opening the botched and badly stitched seams with one's own discoveries and knowledge, then the responsibility to act on that history becomes absolute.

The breakdown of Quentin Compson is, in part, the breakdown of delusion, the breakdown of the old language, the codes, the displacements, the fetishes, the stubborn distancing, othering techniques. The master narrative, with its technique of domination and delusion, of usurpation and definition, will no longer hold. The search for a new language to say these things, for new images to represent these things is the substance of Shreve and Quentin's conversation. They find no new language and the image that emerges of whited-out rabbits, bleached birds in snow-covered tundras is inhuman, closed, frozen, indistinguishable, and undistinguished. But this is Shreve's view, and he may not be the one to give us the most reliable version of things Africanist. After all, when it comes to black people, he cannot even count. [*READ p. 470*] Charles Bon is not two people; he is just one. Charles Bon's name figures in each of the pairs Shreve mentions, and excluding Charles's grandmother, who is not a Sutpen, there are five black Sutpens mentioned and three white ones.

Furthermore, Shreve's vision of the future of Africanist people is self-serving. When he describes them, he uses the language of harmless animals and the vital and complete erasure of color; visibility ("so they won't show up so sharp against the snow"). But when he associates *himself* with Africanism, says "in a few thousand years" the merge will be complete and *he* is part of the merging, the language is suddenly not animalistic. He finds himself "sprung from the loins of African kings." Of course, kings.

A more reliable Ike McCaslin has to put the history as ledger back together, to try to make sense of it. But when he returns to the Edenesque, race-free Big Woods, he finds Boon (not Bond) crazily destroying his gun while he defends its separated disconnected dysfunctional parts.

The second approach, the use of Africanism to disguise class under the rubric of whiteness, should clarify much of Faulkner's work. Let me first say something about Faulkner's critical reputation. His rise is attributed to the critical school that began as Agrarian, then became known principally as the Fugitive Poets. These scholars became the founders of the New Criticism (John Crowe Ransom, Allen Tate, Cleanth Brooks, etc.). They were Southern, conservative scholars rewriting and revising the South after the second catastrophe the South had: the Great Depression. The project of these scholars was to revise Southern mythology, and move it from the celebration of the planter aristocrat to the enfranchisement and elevation of the yeoman—the sturdy, morally responsible yeoman farmer. In order to withstand the Northern attacks on the South as an intellectual and moral "wasteland," the Agrarians and the later Fugitive Poets, along with the innovators of the New Criticism, attacked the stereotype of the aristocratic planter and substituted an image more in line with populist historicism. Yet this new yeoman image is suffused with cavalierism as an ideal. Both the New Critics of the forties and Faulkner shared a distrust of industrialism, and a nostalgia for what had come to be mythologized as the antebellum chivalric code of honor. But Faulkner attempts and succeeds at a persistent critique of so-called southern chivalry (although he is personally guilty of yearning for its accoutrements and its myth of honor). Whatever his personal vanities and pretensions and whatever his depressingly and conventionally racist public utterances, Faulkner the writer engaged in the process of demystification of planter aristocracy and his project, unlike that of the New Critics, was the re-telling and recreating of legend as an expression of *present* needs. His narrative struggle is to come to terms with the now. Thus he began to focus more and more on the rise not of the yeoman but of the poor white class. Consequently, the critical appraisal of his work enforced a "great/late" division. Up to *Absalom, Absalom!* his works are great, with *Absalom! Absalom!* being the apogee. After that, when he concentrates on poor whites, and their relationships with blacks, the work is labeled "late" or "later," meaning lesser. This division in critical appraisal missed or misread an important point. Faulkner is less interested in the Old South, more interested in modern Southern narratives. For the modern South, class plays a decisive role, and since it is formulated in antagonism to blackness, race is part of the equation.

Thomas Sutpen comes from a marginal class; he is like an Africanist character. [Indistinguishable—except for beard—from his slaves (as he works on house)—he is arrested without charge by vigilantes.] He is not even racist in the classic sense as Rosa is (fights with his slaves, is said to have glinting teeth, etc.). "He is not an authentic planter, but a representation of a representation, a sign of that very simplification of the past that was symptomatic of the Southerner's obsessive mythologizing." Rosa's effort is to enter that class; to move from lower middle class pretensions and desire to the aristocracy. Her

narrative is full of the things she does not know about the genealogy of Sutpen; it is disruptive—imposes its own truth—but does
not itself permit interruption; it shows a marked inability to carry a
grammatical progression beyond an initial assertion. Wash, the poor
white, destroys this representation of a representation of class privilege, because of class outrage. The danger for this poor white man is
being treated like a nigger. The nature of Sutpen's demise at the hands
of a poor white is significant, and we should remember that the story
of Wash was at the beginning of Faulkner's contemplation of this
novel. Poor whites throw trash at Sutpen and Ellen when they are
married. They throw it while he is surrounded by protecting blacks;
blacks shielding the bride and her aunt. The wedding is at night,
the black men light the way; the whites do not attend. Beginning
with the marriage rite, the poor white and lower middle class makes
its appearance which culminates in the last birth rite, where Wash
realizes that without "whiteness," that is, the response to blackness,
he and Sutpen are separated by an unbridgeable chasm. When the
black midwife leaves, Wash annihilates his house, his line, and runs,
scythe held high above his head, into the posse, the lanterns, the
guns. [p. 364]

The third approach, the struggle against chaos, is shown to be a
misdirected, dehumanized struggle against internal anarchy as well
as social. The response to chaos is to name, to order, to convince,
and, in so doing, to be willing to violate: land, family members and
connections, Christian traditions, moral rectitude, inheritances, and
ultimately the self. "A community of speakers and listeners solid-
ifies its own corporate identity and . . . authority by repeating a
series of highly figured stories that approximate 'reality' even if the
'real' narrative depends upon rampant misinformation or multiple
omissions. . . . Faulkner traces the mind's tragic irresolution between
the organizing polarities of society and the integrative needs of the
self. The emphasis through his language on the moment of merging
suggests a radical attempt to reintegrate, at least in linguistic terms,

what society had sundered." In its violent response to chaos, Faulkner raises, therefore, the possibility of stillness—revising society, and its hierarchies—and of completing the gap-ridden narrative of history.

The chaos Faulknerian characters react to is social. The national chaos of the Civil War is transferred to domestic chaos represented by Africans. The need for stability, in the face of this social chaos, produces anxiety, encourages classification and rank, linguistic dissemination of these hierarchies and rationales by way of repetitive and re-enforcing speech and discontinuous written documents, real violence or its threat, and the effacement of the process itself: the anxiety, the enforcement, the discontinuity, the violence—all are denied or evaded as long as possible, and when made unavoidable frequently lead to madness, death, social exclusion, or paralysis.

We have to ask, however, what are the risks? The risks of a coherent history, of an integrated self, of a continuous (not disconnected, discontinuous) narrative. The possibility of retribution? of judgment? The probability of aggression—resurfacing as violent domination or as self-destruction? The recognition of defeat? These dangers are all addressed in Faulkner's works, as in few others. But he also forces us to muse over what might be the benefits of stillness to a coherent history. A history that puts back the omissions, the gaps; that dispenses with polarities and divisions, erasures, lapses, forgetfulness. Is the American self doomed to the fate of exchangeable dominances? Is the invention of a pristine past repeated and held on to in order to sustain a segregated, divided future? Might not language designed to accommodate rather than cloak this Africanist presence free us to take a position regarding the deceptions perpetrated upon us? Might it also suggest not "interchangeability" but alterability?

These and other questions have exercised and confounded Faulkner readers for decades. What seems most significant, among these issues, is the clearly self-referential focus of Faulkner's work. The fact that Africanist personae do not enable the text (though it may enable the characters); it is not surrogacy (although surrogate selves are a part of the makeup of many Faulknerian characters); it is not the capture of an Africanist narrative or story for the author's own drama of self-denial (as in Styron's novel, where "othering" is achieved by the persistent, repetitive documentation of visibility, and substituting self into the Other's escape and capture narrative), and although Faulkner's characters explore and exploit an endless variety of serviceable Africanist bodies, the text, unlike Gertrude Stein's, more like Willa Cather's, explores the explorers, and some of the serviceable bodies escape the rigidity of social difference to the wilderness where some other hierarchy applies, and some of them like Charles Bon return to haunt and to challenge and to lay claim before they die. [*Jim Bond passage.*]

What we are suddenly aware of is the absence of mockery, the absence of denigrating language, the presence of language possibilities, the absence of literary exploitation on the part of the author. The differences are there, the barriers—but the estranging distances are those of the protagonists, not those of the text. This is not because Faulkner has some clue to Africanist narrative, idiom, and persona that other writers do not have, or that he is free of all the estranging devices and fatalism of other authors vis-à-vis black people's past and present. Where this dissolution of estrangement occurs, where the history, the narrative, the persona of Africanism is merged with the history, the narrative, the persona of whiteness, where the seams are stitched together, the two complement each other, alter each other. It occurs when language does not permit itself certain kinds of evasions, is not defending a specific reality, but allows itself to become vulnerable to varieties of it.

Nadine Gordimer said, "Cultural identity is the ground on which the exploration of the self in the imaginative writer's hands makes a national literature." If that is the case, we don't really have a completely national literature. Yet. [*This is a repeat from earlier.*]

In our final view of Thomas Sutpen as the patriarchal side of the American formulation of "self," we can measure him against the characteristics American literature has accumulated: innocence; authority; individualism; status through difference.'

1. Innocence. Now we see in Faulkner's narrative what this American is innocent of: "the violence upon which his identity lies," and the "flaw" in his design.

2. Authority. Sutpen has the power of life and death over his slaves; he can control, deny, and repress them. But all of his efforts to erase them fail. His authority is seen to flounder in precisely racial terms: nobody seems to do what Sutpen wants. He has a lot of trouble getting anybody other than the blacks to do what he commands or wishes. Henry refuses his birthright—does not marry or reproduce himself; Eulalia lies or misleads him; Ellen is not the kind of wife he wants; Bon refuses to abandon his engagement; Rosa refuses to marry him; and Wash, the groveling lower-class drinking companion, refuses Sutpen all he has left—his life. Some authority.

3. Individualism. Like the classic "individual" Sutpen is minus a meaningful history, self-made; basks in masculine solitude; has weak personal relationships. If we look closely at these attributes of individualism they too, in *Absalom, Absalom!*, are dependent on or closely associated with Africanist persona or discourse.

    a) being without origin, timeless, historyless is stereotypical assumption of Africanism

    b) his "self-made" achievement is fake: it was ignited by a black servant refusing him entrance into a patriarch's house, and it was realized by black labor

    c) his out-of-the-house masculine solitude periods are primarily shared with blacks in displays of black physical prowess—and Sutpen's competition with them; his longest masculine pursuit is the Civil War which clearly had Afr. as its text.

d) weak personal relationships—no consistent community of whites to which he repairs; probably one single long dialogue with a white man of status (the elder Compson)—the rest of what he says without command or rancor is to blacks: "Ah, Clytie" when back from the War; the conversation with a black woman about the horse over Wash's granddaughter's head. (And it is amazing, as Snead reminds us, how absent these white fathers are: hiding in attics for years; gone to war; etc.)

e) status—propertied or unpropertied—is dependent on a class of people called blacks. As Wash so clearly realizes, Wash who is treated like a nigger, and who is even ridiculed by niggers for being like them, he is nothing without the struts and support system of Africanist discourse. What, [James] Snead asks, would Rosa or any of these people be without a class called "nigger"? Well, they might *be* niggers, and the fear and threat of merging into blackness propels the project that is the genius of *Absalom, Absalom!*, propels the project that is Southern; the project that is American.

Next week, in Bellow's *Henderson the Rain King*, we will look at that American experience when the fear of merging collapses and the protagonist *chooses* to merge.

Saul Bellow

Last week I made an attempt to subject Faulkner's novel *Absalom, Absalom!* to four of the approaches to American Africanism that were discussed in this series of lectures. These approaches represent a few of the ways in which we can see how needed a black presence is in the construction of white, that is to say American, literature. And to see how that need is unacknowledged, recognized, and exploited. I discussed the deployment of Africanist discursive practice; the kind of linguistic strategies Faulkner uses and critiques. Then the use of race as a disguise for other kinds of difference, other kinds of internal divisions—such as class divisions, and gender differences—how much Faulkner reveals to us about the frailty of white patriarchy when race is removed from its construction of itself. In this regard I referred to a sophisticated version of the minstrel strategy—the presence of blacks providing license for whites and a joining mechanism between warring white factions. Third, I discussed the use of blacks as the means by which chaos is negotiated—the practice of associating anarchy, disorder, illegality, and so on with blackness; how naming and violence figure in the response to this perceived chaos, and how the possibilities of stillness are raised in Faulkner's work as alternatives.

What I didn't have time to do is conclude the lecture with some suggestions of how this novel through its protagonist points to some of the defining characteristics of the American "self" and to very pronounced repetitive themes in American literature. Innocence. Individualism. Authority (meaning virility and power). Difference (meaning claims of status and rights of authenticity through hierarchical positions of difference).

In our final view of Thomas Sutpen, the patriarchal side of the American formulation of "self" is revealed as containing all of these attributes.

1. Innocence. We are able to detect in Faulkner's narrative what this particular and representative American claims to be innocent of. One is that he is innocent of "the violence upon which his identity lies." Another is that he claims to be innocent of a moral system complex enough to identify his error; to recognize that his "flaw," his "mistake" is not a piece left out of a puzzle, nor hairline crack on an otherwise perfect crystal. It is the very material of which his plans were made that is insupportable.

That Thomas Sutpen, Quentin Compson, Rosa, major characters in the novel, are racked by the necessity for defending earlier positions rather than analyzing them, taking them on—they appear to be beyond spiritual or intellectual help because they are unable to learn anything new. Racism is interesting in that way—it can be used for almost anything except for developing something new; it requires stasis, it requires constant gestures of conservation; it can only invent the wheel one more time. Thus the weariness at the heart of a discourse that cannot hear itself, can only search for its raison d'être—the Africanism that purifies, baptizes, and enforces an American innocence that criticism is too polite to itself to call—American ignorance.

2. Authority. Thomas Sutpen has the power of life and death over his slaves. He can own, control, deny, and oppress them. And since he seems unable to get anybody other than the blacks to do what he says, to obey ultimately his authority, it appears that the authority was borrowed, as it were. Or perhaps even lent for a while. Certainly it looked real. Once, however, the absolute control over the lives of the blacks is removed, we see that such power is intrinsically helplessness. Henry refuses his birthright; does not marry or reproduce himself. Eulalia lies or misleads Sutpen. Ellen dies. Bon refuses to abandon his engagement to Judith. Rosa Coldfield refuses to marry him. And Wash, the groveling drinking companion, squatter, and handyman, refuses Sutpen all he has left—his life.

The question begs attention. How much of the authority and power construed as the patriarch's is the roar and mane of a toothless, clawless lion?

3. Individualism. Like the classic "individual" Sutpen is minus a meaningful history. He is a self-made man basking in masculine solitude. He has necessarily weak personal relationships which are displaced or dismissed or disregarded, for he is complete within himself. If we look closely at these attributes of individualism as represented in Thomas Sutpen, they are dependent on or closely associated with Africanist persona and/or discourse.

   a) being without origin, timeless, historyless is stereotypical assumption about black people in literature. The dichotomy is that they are seen (as Gertrude Stein said) [as] both "ancient" and sufferers from "nothing"; the contradiction is implicit: they are the oldest people on earth and the ones for whom history has no place nor meaning. This Africanist attribute of being without a past is transferred to Sutpen. This association, layered onto Blacks, becomes systemic in the American character that claimed itself always new, renewable, and unrestrained by any history, especially his own.

b) his masculine solitude periods are primarily shared with blacks in displays of physical prowess. His longest masculine pursuit is in the Civil War, which clearly has Africanism as its text.

c) distant and weak personal relationships. For Sutpen there seems to be no consistent community of whites to which he repairs. Other than one single long dialogue with a white man of status (the elder Compson) the rest of what he says without command or rancor is to blacks. And it is amazing, as Snead says, how absent these white fathers are: hiding in attics, gone to war, locked in bedrooms.

d) status, propertied or unpropertied, this status is dependent on a class of people called blacks. As Wash so clearly realizes, Wash, who is treated "like a nigger," and who is even ridiculed by them for being like them, is nothing without the struts and support system of Africanist discourse. What would Rosa or any of these people be without a class called "nigger"? Whatever it is, and it might be something wonderful, we won't ever know. Because they are locked in whiteness; because behind the search for Blackness is the threat of merging into blackness that is what propels the project that is the genius of *Absalom, Absalom!;* propels the project that is Southern; the project that is American.

In Saul Bellow's *Henderson the Rain King* we will look at that American experience when the fear of merging collapses and the protagonist chooses to merge.

When we read Saul Bellow, we are reading the work of a writer terribly interested in the process of becoming an American, interested also in transcending (in some cases, transforming) ethnic, regional, and racial boundaries. This effort at transcendence is quite explicit in *Henderson the Rain King,* where the protagonist, telling his own story, is furiously chasing something that could be described as a "free human existence." Free of the restraint and the burdens that the best of Western culture and materiality have to offer, and "human" in the sense of being, feeling, and claiming no allegiance to or dependency on any of the cultural formations that can limit him. A "human" life, in this sense, is a decidedly ahistorical one; a non-racist one. It would seem inevitable then that the journey in search of the fundamental, the liberated self take place in Africa. Perhaps for the reasons mentioned earlier—Africa is both ancient and nothing; blank and full of meaning and inscription.

Bellow's Africa is genuinely Africanist, that is, symbolically, metaphorically, discursively black. He has no intention of describing Africa or Africans in any but a Western textbook fashion, or of learning from whatever indigenous knowledge they may have. He is in fact working out Western knowledge (psychiatry, social studies, poetry, and philosophy) on them and through them. The question, then, is what is it about Africa or Africanism that makes this the desirable site for this major journey from disease into health, from misery into happiness, from self-loathing into self-love?

I'm going to rely on a critic's perceptive reading of *Henderson,* then intervene into that critique with certain additional lines of reading that come from our study in this course. Eusebio L. Rodrigues's book *The Quest for the Human* is the complete and most exhaustive of these readings. [*READ Rodrigues, p. 108, 1st para.*]

Before we say anything else we should note the terms of this description of Bellow's enterprise: "Self-authenticity"; lavish abandon is coupled with control, tame the turbulent, obedient to the commands, and the *descent* (going to Africa is understood as a step down, a descent into backwardness) "into the heart of darkness returning not with horror, but a radiant confidence in man and human possibility." We have to wonder what makes this abandon possible if not the associative values of Africanistic stereotyping: the association of savagery, blankness, historyless, the absence of restraint, the serviceability, the limitless love and so on? Rodrigues's critical language is suffused with references to this Africanistic utility.

According to Rodrigues, the full power of Bellow's novel is available to us only if we are aware of its intertextuality. Primarily William Blake, and William Reich, but also Hemingway, T. S. Eliot, Dreiser, and Salinger. For the anthropological information about African cultural practices, Bellow depended on Melville Herskovits (with whom he studied at Northwestern). Bellow had not visited Africa when this novel was written. So, on the one hand, Africa is Bellow's own imaginative construct, but on the other, it is based on Western anthropology and fused with his own imaginative purposes in order to discover the limits of human imagination—its sources as well as its regenerative power.

Let us look at some of the intertextual references. First, the references to other authors. These references are usually put-downs that tell us what Bellow is criticizing, what displeases him about the "state of the world" in the fifties.

"Bellow launches an attack against Hemingway with the missile of laughter. The Hemingway attitude to life is unmercifully pilloried and parodied. Bellow boldly tacks on the Hemingway initials, E.H., to the name of his protagonist. Henderson pours bourbon in his morning coffee from a big flask—and then spends the day on the beach smashing bottles with a plywood slingshot. He goes to the wilds of Africa armed with a powerful .375 H&H Magnum rifle, but tamely surrenders it to the Wariri. Bellow pours ridicule upon the Hemingway mystique that hunting is a way of achieving grace: "'Myself, I used to have a certain interest in hunting, but as I grew older it seemed a strange way to relate to nature. What I mean is, a man goes into the external world, and all he can do with it is to shoot it? It doesn't make sense.'" (The interesting phrase here is "the external world.")

"Like Holden Caulfield, the protagonist of Salinger's *The Catcher in the Rye* . . . Henderson affects a red wool hunting cap which he wears at all times and on all occasions. Holden wears his cap to proclaim his eccentric defiance of the hypocritical world he lives in; for Henderson, however, the cap merely keeps his head in one piece. Holden dreams of saving all the children in the world; Henderson merely pulls down the bill of his cap to hide his embarrassment when he hears the cries of his foundling daughter." (The interesting item for us here is the color/race of this foundling.)

"Bellow dismisses Henry Adams's nostalgia for a lost unity that can never be recaptured. Henderson visits the cathedral towns of France, where the religion and beauty of the churches enthrall him . . . but they do not satisfy his demands, and he gets drunk in every one of them: in Chartres, home of Adams's virgin, he threatens his wife Lily with suicide.

"Bellow also rejects Dreiser's theory of social Darwinism. Henderson's visit to the aquarium at Banyules, where he stares at an octopus, deliberately echoes the opening of *The Financier*, where Frank Cowperwood fascinatedly watches a lobster gradually eat up a squid . . .

"More basic is Bellow's total rejection of Eliot, whom he regards as the chieftain of the contemporary prophets of doom and despair. *Henderson the Rain King* is a massive counterblast at the fears of the apocalypse generated by *The Waste Land*. Against the mythic figure of the impotent, paralytic Fisher King, Bellow opposes the Rain King, as the embodiment of power and motion. On his way back from Providence, Rhode Island, Henderson plays solitaire not with a Tarot pack, but with an ordinary deck of cards which keep falling on the floor . . . muttering helplessly: 'There is a curse on this land. There is something bad going on. Something is wrong. There is a curse on this land.'" "Henderson pokes fun at Eliot's Christian nightingale, whose message is that mankind cannot bear too much reality. But how much unreality can humankind stand, asks Henderson." "So what if reality may be terrible. It's better than what we've got."

"The voice, the cry that Henderson hears from deep within, 'I want, I want,' is Bellow's central metaphor, unifies the major themes in *Henderson the Rain King*. The words that the voice speaks have been taken from *The Gates of Paradise*, the emblem book that Blake created in order to lead man to true vision. Plate 9 of this guide to Paradise shows us a man crying out at the foot of a long ladder that reaches up to the moon: 'I want! I want!' Henderson, Bellow suggests, is a Blakean pilgrim, mankind itself, caught in the grip of a boundless desire for a new and vital life. The voice is also a cry from the depths of Henderson's true being, a desperate plea for self-fulfillment." (The operative word for us is self-fulfillment.)

"Henderson's voice is also a seriocomic dramatization of the central premise of Reichian theory, a manifestation of the orgone energy which has been dammed up in Henderson and which now clamors for release. Finally, it is the voice of America itself, a Jeffersonian cry for the renewal and resurrection of the true spirit that had animated America in the past."

These references of dismissal and acknowledgment help us know what Bellow is suspicious of or what he dismisses completely as the pervading problem and view of "modern," that is, 1950s Western, civilization.

So, where to go to discover fundamental truths about Western civilization? To Africa. There Bellow imposes on and re-creates by and through this invented Africa the parts of Western wisdom that seem to him to apply—Reichean psychoanalytic theory and practice among them.

William Reich studied with Freud and struck out, as many of his students did, on his own with a radical theory and practice of psychoanalysis. Regarded as a bit daft, he is back in favor in some quarters today, and you should recognize some of his principles of orgone therapy: "Orgone therapy destroys the muscular armor, to reestablish plasma mobility, and to dissolve the attitude of holding back. The human body can be divided into seven segments (ocular, oral, neck, chest, diaphragmatic, abdominal and pelvic) separated by armor rings at right angles to the spine. The orgone energy streams longitudinally from the center of the organism along the body axis, but is inhibited by the armor rings that block the orgonotic streams. The orgonotic current flows from the tail end over the back to the head, and then runs backward over the chest and abdomen toward the genitals. . . . According to Reich, 'since the body of the patient is held back and since the goal of orgone therapy is that of reestablishing the plasmatic currents in the pelvis, it is necessary to start the dissolution of the armor in the regions farthest away from the pelvis. Thus, the work begins with the facial expressions.' . . . The face of Henderson, with its various colors, its mobility, its expressiveness, and its distortions, is the biological region where the energy, especially in the form of aggressive rage, manifests itself clearly." "Any inhibited aggressive rage . . . directs the energy toward the musculature of the peripheral extremities where it becomes manifest." "So Henderson wants to 'seize the whole building in my mouth and bite it in two, as Moby Dick had done to the boats.'" "Teeth constitute the oral segment of the muscular armor. The breakdown of this segment marks the first stage of the dissolution of Henderson's armored condition." Apparently all of Henderson's physiognomy and its symptoms can be traced to Reich's orgone therapy, and note that Bellow was an admirer of Reich (although he believed he went too far). With this in mind we can note the comparison of Henderson with Queen Willatale: ". . . she has no pathological armor." In Reichian terms. Supple forehead, that radiant smile, the harmony of her body, the happy light in her eye. "Good nature emanated from her; it seemed to puff out on her breath as she sat smiling." Etc. She gives him three pieces of wisdom: You heart barking; world is strange to a child; grun-tu-molani man want to live.

When Henderson lifts Mummah, he has moved a center of orgone energy, an old woman who "was a living personality, not an idol." And after he lifts her his armor blocks explode.

Even the rainmaking is Reichian. For Reich believed that "one may create clouds in the cloud free sky . . . by disturbing the evenness in the distribution of the atmospheric OR energy; thus clouds appear upon drawing energy from the air." (Thus the sexual language when the rainmakings take place—genital primacy of orgone therapy.) In 1952 Reich demonstrated that it was possible both to create clouds and to destroy them to produce rain. Perhaps the most sweepingly ambitious of his ideas was the . . . Upanishadic THE SAME ENERGY WHICH GOVERNS THE MOVEMENTS OF ANIMALS AND THE GROWTH OF ALL LIVING SUBSTANCES ALSO ACTU-ALLY MOVES THE HEAVENLY BODIES.

King Dahfu, therefore, is Bellow's embodiment of the ideas of William Reich: physically loose, relaxed, noble, vigorous . . . "with sexual charm" which "goes with a relaxed musculature and free-flowing psychic activity. The rhythm of the motions, . . . combines with modulation in speech." Dahfu's face is not armored; it slopes forward, it isn't held back, his eyes are huge, soft, eccentric—not like Henderson's tunnel-like eyes, they gleam with a soft light; there is a continuous smile on his lips which are large, red, and tumid, and on his head, hair did not grow, it lived. "He seemed all at ease, and I all limitation. He was extended, floating; I was contracted and cramped. The undersides of my knees were sweating. Yes, he was soaring like a spirit while I sank like a stone." In fact, according to Rodrigues, the climax of the novel, and its complete process, can be read as the Wil-liam Reichian therapy fulfilled through King Dahfu—after certain preliminary circumstances have been met. At that point, Henderson can understand the three pieces of wisdom Queen Willatale gave him: the physical constriction of his heart (love yearning blocked) has been removed—he loves now and understands the love of other people; he sees the wonder and magic of the physical universe (like a child) but is not fearful of it or its strangeness; and though he wants to live, he has encountered death and, therefore, can live. Fully.

Although Henderson is presented to us as out of control, Bellow is very much in control. That is, controlling the information that is pertinent, shaping it to reveal Western concerns, and Western solutions. The Africans are both mirrors of the twentieth-century West and its site of healing. Both doctor and patient. The antagonism between the King and the Bunam is more than a tribal quarrel: it represents the conflict between the reasoning power in man and the human imagination. The Bunam has the look of rationality and death; the leather-winged bat constitutes the specter which was reasoning power in Blake. The Bunam does not want Henderson's little gifts, he wants his signature, looks on the atlas for his home. King Dahfu is the possibility of the human imagination. "Imagination, imagination, imagination! It converts to actual. It sustains, it alters, it redeems!" He even quotes Blake: "The tigers of wrath are wiser than the horses of instruction" (from "The Marriage of Heaven and Hell"). Atti is an agent of Reichean therapy, but also Blake's tiger. Burning bright in the forests of intellectual night. Bellow makes Henderson peer into her eyes as " 'clear circles of inhuman wrath, convex, brown and pure, rings of black light within them.' "

King Dahfu "puts him on the tack to wisdom." " 'Chaos does not run the whole show.' " Human life is definitely not "a sick and hasty ride, helpless, through a dream into oblivion." And "art is one way of meeting chaos." According to Reich, word language and concepts cannot penetrate the pathological depth-forms for expression. To understand one's condition intellectually is not enough. "What Henderson needs is a savage and dynamic form of therapy." This savage and dynamic form is available in context and contact with a programmatically imagined Africanism.

[PART II]

In *Henderson the Rain King* we see the process of becoming other in a form different from Styron's, but in some ways similar to the othering strategies seen in Melville, Stein, Hemingway's *Garden of Eden,* and by inflection in O'Connor. In Styron the self was transferred intact into the body of the other hoping to be invisible there, hoping to be the complete penetration into the mind and body of the other with no referent to the self imagining it. The failure of that enterprise makes up a great deal of the criticism of that book. Here with Henderson, the self is aggressively, powerfully *visible.* But its visibility is possible *only when it merges with the other* (that is, touches it, lives as it does, thinks like the Other, and most importantly *feels* like the other as well as *for* the other). That merging process is equated with the discovery of "reality."

Bellow's explicit search is for life; his implicit search is for the death encounter. Therefore the death of his Africanistic friend is an opportunity for Henderson to love, and to consume and survive the experience. It is important to remember that Bellow associates Henderson with the American, the Everyman—and this everyman's entanglement with Africa as an allegory for the past, present, and future of America.

We have also seen Bellow deploy the weapons of a specific formulation of Western psychiatric methods—those of William Reich—to develop the narrative and the growth of his protagonist.

The imaginative, creative problem of the novel is to use one set of weapons to demolish another set. To engage the author's own armory of potentially liberating Western learning with his character's store of inhibiting weaponry. [*Comic mode, etc. READ p. 109*]

The question then becomes why is not Bellow's armor of Western thought sufficient for this job in Danbury, Connecticut, or in New York or in Paris? What is there about the site (Africa) that makes the exchange of weaponry, this clash of weaponry possible in a way in which it would not be elsewhere?

First of all, Western weapons are in disarray; they are disparate, in diaspora, and seemingly conflicting. They are also, at the time of the writing of this book, death-loving. The problem is to disentangle the learning; to order, hone the weapons, to select the most efficient ones and discard the obsolete.

Second of all, Bellow needed a certain kind of protagonist. [p. 113] If Henderson and Bellow are to get to the heart of the disease (the twentieth century illness), they must not be distracted—distracted by pressures that are trivial, that fructify emotional learning. They must also be free to pursue the cure without being stopped: jailed, hospitalized, killed (by others or the self); and they must not be hindered in this pursuit by being dismissed and marginalized as eccentric, unserious (comic), or socially dangerous. It is of paramount interest that these obstacles to the pursuit of health and happiness: distraction by pressures that are beside the point or trivial; pressures that freeze cognitive and emotional learning; routine confrontation with barriers to the pursuit of freedom (possibility of institutionalization, incarceration, marginalization, dismissal as eccentric, comic and/or socially dangerous)—all of these obstacles are both applicable to Henderson's predicament and associated with the life situation of African-Americans in the United States.

We can say with some safety that Bellow Africanizes Henderson's situation and places him in an Africanized context to underscore the point. [p. 114]

In Africa, and Africa alone, can Henderson's weapons be freely exchanged, honed, and put to their most efficient and constructive use. Why? Why Africa? That is the question that opens the book [*READ*] and is never fully explained. Because Africa is a site where definitions about freedom can take place. Not a realistic Africa, rather a fantastic one. Henderson needs a certain kind of judgment-free environment. An environment where he can meet all of the dangers of 20th century life without the consequences of those dangers. The formulation of Henderson's problems are made in three areas: eros, thanatos, and clio (love/sex, death, and history). Henderson can walk away from the cistern fiasco; he has the immediate and loyal services of a black body, a guide and protector without whom he would have died. He can confront his own death *through* the imminent death of his friend King Dahfu. He can become intimate and *like* a lioness under the watchful and protective eye of the King himself. Where in a modern city or even in a modern rural area can a man press his face into a female navel outside of a clinic or a brothel without the pressure of a confining psychiatric illness and without pornographic implications? Where can he feel love for the power of women without the ropes and bindings of marriage or an affair or an erotic entanglement? Where else but in a wholly imagined Africa can one meditate on the origins of things without having to engage the social and political history that followed those origins? Eden after the fall, but without reference to what precipitated the fall.

Africa (in historical fact and in imaginative assumption) has already fallen. We take that for granted, believe it, because we know what, in the 20th century, it has been subjected to for four previous centuries (conquest, exploitation, etc.). We know that it is an available place for missionaries, helpers, people who want to do good—freely, without help or interference from those being saved. In other words, one can feel good about oneself there. However terrible or unsavory the missionary may be, the helper/saver may be, his or her work is presumably needed, and there can or will be no negative judgment about character or personality or honor or the interior self. (It is not, presumably, the kind of place where one has to be good to do good; where bad people are prevented from doing good.) So it retains, for literary imaginative purposes, its prior Edenesque characteristics: freedom to act without and before judgment, and its anterior ones:

bereftness, the conditions of having been judged and found wanting, expelled, as it were, from God's grace and mercy.

Africa is both pre- and post-Eden. It is where one can both "get away" and "get to"; escape to and engage with; act out and act on; it is a site both infantilized and matured; both inscribed and erased. It is simultaneously ancient and primary; historicized and timeless. Bellow's Africa is both sophisticated and savage. The question of why the Arnewi have no water available to them is attributed to their curious though touching regard for their cattle. (Like those televised and international efforts to get cadres of Westerners to go to Africa to teach a four-million-year-old race of people how to dig a hole in the ground, or plant a field. The *Charlie and the Chocolate Factory* story.) It is conveniently backward. Conveniently poor. These terms are both true and false. It has been held back, and it is in the nature of the late twentieth century bankrupted language to be able to accurately identify a country with all of the tungsten in the world as poor.

So it is not only fitting that Bellow goes to Africa for this particular journey; it is inevitable. Bellow Africanizes Henderson, and through him becomes the Other, and places him in the location where Othering can safely take place. Thus, the process of Othering (the symbiotic relationship between Henderson and King Dahfu) is undertaken by an already Othered protagonist. Henderson is like a black American. Traveling to Africa (his or her motherland) and *recognizing it*. Since Henderson is offered to us as a representative if not mythic "American," it will occur to us that this 20th-century American Everyman is indisputably, naturally Africanist.

Now perhaps one can understand why it is important for Henderson to take with him the soul of the King and to confront the white silence with such leaps of faith and love—which are his new weapons. He has not only become the Other, he has captured his soul and is enabled, therefore, empowered, to confront the quintessential Africanist problem—confronting the white silence with the weapons selected from and honed in his culture: dance, faith, and love and freedom.

"Since I distrust you, I must understand you."

That sentence reverberates throughout this book; it virtually glows in the dark. Let us add another:

"Since I am you, I understand me."

Henderson appears with fully developed but pathological armor. Armor that must be stripped away if he is to be healed, if he is to be free and to live without fear. He is presented to us as strong, unkillable—but he is not well. He is clearly "free" in the modern, capitalistic sense: he is rich, has a passport, and being white and male, has a certain license—to be wild, make outrageous claims and gestures of defiance; but he is not free in the only valuable sense of the work: psychologically free. Questions are whether and on what terms the becoming Other takes place. What is the meaning of the stolen lion cub in view of the healing that has presumably gone on? Is this, perhaps, a benign cannibalism? Or the missionary zeal that Henderson takes on when he says he wants to be a doctor—in India perhaps? Has Henderson learned anything new about the Africans? If not, and it seems not, the text is wholly and forthrightly self-reflexive. What then does that self-reflection say, not about Henderson, but about the availability of the Africanist presence, what it stirs up in the writer's imagination? Why is Henderson in Africa? Really? Is there any other culture that could help him in his search this way? Why is the language, problematized according to Bellow, less elevated than King Dahfu's? (Its language, its "vocabulary," says Rodrigues, "had to be far-ranging so that Henderson could speak of laughter and lions, of tears and madness, of trivia . . . love, suffering, reality, and nobility, of realistic details in America and of fantastic events in Africa.") [see p. 166]

And if these black Others, these primary, original Others were so helpful, what does the ending suggest: the dance on the frozen runway, the American/Persian orphan, and most of all, the dark faces looking out from within, the pure white lining of the gray Arctic silence? Is this another non sequitur, inescapable, like Poe's? Another white, silent, impenetrable veil? Has Bellow *become* Other? Or has he usurped the Other? Has he, indeed, usurped the process of Othering?

Saul Bellow makes no secret of the self-reflexive properties of his mission. Indeed he is refreshingly forthright. His representative American becomes free, healthy, and capable of love by his imaginative appropriation of the original Africanist Presence—from which and in which he can discover not only what it means to be raceless, but what it means to be human.

Those of you not accustomed to reading literature for new ways of reading may feel some assurance about how neatly this argument has been developed. Those of you accustomed to reading for and along different lines will recognize the neatness and use it, I hope, to develop other designs for critical interventions into American literature. In any case, the plan of this course has been to alert you to the possibilities of an enhanced and richer reading when we relate an art form to the historical world in which it exists.

Appendix

Notes

xiii "peculiar compromise": See James Madison, "Federalist, no. 54," in Alexander Hamilton, James Madison, and John Jay, *The Federalist: A Collection of Essays Written in Favor of the New Constitution, as Agreed upon by the Federal Convention, Sep. 17, 1787 with Letters of "Brutus,"* ed. Terence Ball (Cambridge: Cambridge University Press, 2003), p. 289. Of special interest is that the counter-argument advanced by the abolitionist members of the Continental Congress, in their zeal to punish slaveholding states *both* fiscally and legislatively, was *not* that enslaved persons be counted wholly as persons, but, on the contrary, that they be counted *solely* as property, thereby severely limiting the number of congressional representatives proportionally accorded those states and increasing the newly minted dollar value of the "property"—including that of all humans defined as such—on which they would be obligated to pay federal taxes.

xiv father of all cyborg fantasies: Julien Offray de la Mettrie, *L'Homme Machine* (Leiden: Luzac fils, 1748).

xiv "considered by our laws": Madison, "Federalist, no. 54," p. 265.

xiv British "trading partners": Beginning in 1563, the enormous wealth of the newly created British mercantile class, which would soon ascend to the highest ranks of the government and aristocracy and establish the self-dealing funding for the global imperialism of the Victorian period, owed more to no industry than the royal slave trade. The official abolition of the slave trade in 1807 and the 1833 emancipation of the roughly one million Africans without whose slave labor the largely absentee-owned plantations of the British Caribbean and West Indian colonies would not have existed, let alone fed and clothed the British mainland, extended rather than impeded this self-dealing. Further enriching their compatriots, the British government directed the Bank of England to pay out the equivalent of $20 billion in compensation to slaveholders for the per capita "losses" of "property" they "suffered" due to emancipation. See C. Hall, N. Draper, K. McClelland, K. Donnington, and R. Lang, *Legacies of British Slave Ownership* (Cambridge: Cambridge University Press, 2016); C. Hall, N. Draper, and K. McClelland, *Emancipation and the Remaking of the British Imperial World* (Manchester, UK: Manchester University Press, 2014); and the documentation now officially provided on the UK Parliament website: https://heritagecollections .parliament.uk/stories/the-transatlantic-slave-trade/.

xiv   "the Federal Constitution": Madison, "Federalist, No. 54," p. 265.

xiv   spelled out in the Constitution itself: As discussed in the context of the fictions of William Styron, the historical occlusion of this *singular* dehumanization of the nation's African population and their descendants, despite its explicit stipulation in the laws of the nation, in favor of a purported "universality" of suffering and oppression on the basis of any number of group "identities," is paralleled by revisionist "universalist" narratives lamenting "all the innocent victims of the Holocaust." Passing itself off as all the greater humanism for grieving the fate of afflicted mankind everywhere, such "universal" sympathy not only levels all injuries but sorely misses the point: the constitution of a nation "declaring" "universal" "truths" "to be" "self-evident" simultaneously *singled out one* group of people for exclusion from those truths. Similarly, having campaigned upon a platform of virulent, explicitly race-based scapegoating preceding and unrelated to its persecution of short-lived political opposition, the Nazi regime established itself from the very start as a nationally unifying and then an imperial force, by imposing upon its chosen other a cascade of dehumanizing "racial laws": the banning of Jews from all civil service jobs in 1933; their exclusion from all other arenas of life by the 1935 Nuremberg Race and Reich Citizenship Laws; and, finally, in 1939, orders compelling Jews in every nation it invaded to wear their exclusion literally on their sleeves, to mark themselves publicly as subjects for annihilation by exhibiting at all times an officially designed five-point star defining their very existence as a priori grounds for their roundup, deportation, and enslavement. As the separation, disenfranchisement, and terrorization of the future descendants of enslaved Africans, on no other basis than that their ancestors' politically contrived definition as mere fractions of persons disposable at will, continued to be legally enshrined long *after* the passage of the 14th Amendment to the Constitution intended to make them whole, so the legal groundwork for the policy of industrialized mass genocide posthumously piously misnamed "the Holocaust" (or "burnt sacrifice") of all of Europe's Jewish population and their descendants established itself *alone* and on *no other basis* than that of a present or historical religious affiliation itself designated a "race." In short, along with their unprecedented intergenerational and international reach, these unprecedented actions and conditions are specifically predicated upon *anti*-universality.

xv   Legally redefining: It was the further legal extension to all the "free states" of the "property rights" originally accorded slaveholders within their own states, by the congressional passage of the Fugitive Slave Act of 1850, that Stowe—alone among American novelists—repeatedly lambasts as a "legislative" abomination in *Uncle Tom's Cabin.*

xviii   "the color line": Frederick Douglass, "The Color Line," *North American Review* 132, no. 295 (June 1881): 567–577.

xviii   theorists of the ideological underpinnings: Among these last, to name only the most historically significant: the great founder of dialectical literary criticism, Georg Lukács; the preeminent cultural critics of the Frankfurt School, T. W. Adorno and Herbert Marcuse; and the leading American Marxist literary critic, Frederic Jameson.

xviii   subjectively "malleable": G. W. F. Hegel, *Aesthetics. Lectures on Fine Art,* trans. T. M. Knox, 2 vols. (1835; Oxford, UK: Clarendon Press, 1998), 2:972.

xviii   every language is: Jean-Jacques Rousseau, *Discourse on the Origin and Foundations of Inequality Among Men,* trans. Victor Gourevitch (1755; Cambridge: Cambridge University Press, 2016); Ferdinand de Saussure, *Course in General Linguistics,* trans. Roy Harris (1916; London: Bloomsbury, 2013); Emmanuel Levinas, *Otherwise Than Being* (1974; Pittsburgh: Duquesne University Press, 1995).

xix   "discourse": Morrison, p. 150.

xix   "Had I not": Morrison, p. 67.

xx   private and state-sponsored companies: The generic "negro" (from the Latin *nigrum*) was first coined by the private Portuguese and Spanish companies that inaugurated the *transatlantic* method of slave trade in the fifteenth century. Rapidly adopted and expanded by monarchies across Europe, this new triangular routing of commercial profits back to the empires from which they sprang was in turn sanctified by a series of papal bulls bestowing upon Catholic rulers the divine right to enslave all African and indigenous island peoples in perpetuity, by reason of the eternal damnation to which their non-Christianity had already condemned them. Cf. Herbert S. Klein and Jacob Klein, *The Transatlantic Slave Trade* (Cambridge: Cambridge University Press, 1999); William Phillips, *Slavery in Medieval and Early Modern Iberia* (Philadelphia: University of Pennsylvania Press, 2014); Arlindo Caldeira, "Portuguese Slave Trade," in *The Oxford Research Encyclopedia of African History* (2024: https://doi.org/10.1093/acrefore/9780190277734.013.903).

xx   All forms of insult: See J. L. Austin, *How to Do Things with Words,* ed. J. O. Urmson and Marina Sbisa (Cambridge, MA: Harvard University Press, 1975).

xxi   "illocutionary act": Austin, *How to Do Things,* p. 99: "the performance of an illocutionary act, i.e., the performance of an act *in* saying something as opposed to the performance of an act *of* saying something."

xxii   neutral statement of fact: Austin dubs this kind of "report" of reality a "constative statement," in contrast to the active interventions in reality committed by performative statements. Such a report of self-evident truth is precisely the role perversely assigned the title of O'Connor's story by the character who proclaims it out loud. As alluded to above, the character in question is a poor white man who, the story goes, has chosen to visit Atlanta with his son in order to educate him in the horrors of the "big" (i.e., racially mixed) "city."

Spatially disoriented as soon as he leaves the train station and increasingly lost and embarrassed at every turn, the man exults in finally encountering and naming as such the grotesquely "artificial" embodiment of a classic trope of black servitude, the black-faced, diminutive "lawn jockey" still adorning private properties across the U.S. today. Disfigured and discolored in its every feature, its unattended state of dilapidation suggesting its fall from fashion with its current owners, the timeworn figure provides an immediate source of relief and reassurance of the "reality" of "race" that his and his son's actual experience had even more disorientingly refuted. For worse than their disorientation in space is the estranging sense of intimidation they felt in well-to-do white neighborhoods and the surprising absence of intimidation they felt in the city's integrated downtown and black neighborhoods, all livelier, more accommodating, and, above all, communicative than the unyielding, woodlands isolation in which the father believed this trip would convince his son to remain. As Morrison's lecture on the story makes clear, the father's declared constative of reality works only because it doesn't pertain to reality at all: "the artificial nigger" is instead just what its designator desperately needs it to be, the revolting concrete emblem of a race nowhere to be found elsewhere.

xxii   "construct": Morrison, p. 153.

xxiii "If race cannot be *seen*": Morrison, p. 150 [original emphasis].

xxiv   "self-legislating": Immanuel Kant, "Preface" to the *Critique of Pure Reason* (2nd ed. 1782); *Critique of Practical Reason* (1788).

xxiv   as Jean-Jacques Rousseau: Preceding the American Revolution and the Declaration of Independence by over two decades, this is the core principle of Rousseau's revolutionary political, no less than epistemological, thesis in his *Discourse on the Origin and Foundations of Inequality Among Men* (1754; pub. 1755); his definition there, as in his later *Social Contract* (1762), is of freedom as the single internal condition defining all human beings, which, because it is "moral" or existential rather than "physical" or circumstantial, can be externally materially constrained but never removed or "alienated" from our mind's abilities. Rousseau, like Kant following him, would extend that inalienability to whole nations, categorically denying the right of any people to enslave any other. Kant included the appropriation of any people's land or property under that prohibition in his *Metaphysic of Morals* (1792).

xxv   American "experiment": George Washington, First Inaugural Address, New York City, April 30, 1789.

xxvi   America itself as a "Dark House": Polk relates Faulkner's insistent conception of "the Dark House" to which his characters fatally cling with the haunted "Gothic mansions of Poe and the British and American literary traditions" (*Children of the Dark House*, p. 29). Morrison, pp. 144–151.

xxvi   One allegorical figure: Cited by Morrison in her lecture on Faulkner, James Snead's *Figures of Division: William Faulkner's Major Novels* (London: Methuen, 1986) provides a pathbreaking analysis of Faulkner's critical employment of *literary* "figures of division," specifically so as to underscore their real-life contradiction. See esp.: "It seems the mind uses various figures of division to defend itself against chaos—figures which, however, seem only to reintroduce it. Faulkner's genealogical obsession resembles, yet ultimately contradicts, Southern segregationist logic which seeks racially pure pedigrees in the past. Faulkner's genealogical research discovers not purity but rather merging and chaos, states against which the traditions of social classification and division vainly struggle" (p. 7).

xxvi As Morrison reveals: See Morrison, pp. 144–145.

xxvi this was the title Faulkner: In *Children of the Dark House: Text and Context in Faulkner*, Neal Polk calls attention to the lasting significance of that ultimately rescinded title in Faulkner's mind based on a careful study of the tens of thousands of manuscript and typescript pages, straight down to the changes in handwriting in the former, and punctuation in the latter, that Faulkner himself preserved. See Neal Polk, *Children of the Dark House: Text and Context in Faulkner* (Jackson: University of Mississippi Press, 1996), chap. 1, "Where the Comma Goes: Editing Faulkner," pp. 3–21, and the eponymous chap. 2, "Children of the Dark House," pp. 22–98, which, opening with Faulkner's evident recall of Dickens's *Bleak House,* proceeds to provide a Freudian, primarily Oedipal-based reading of the meaning of "darkness" in Faulkner's imagination, offering that though "I will view [Faulkner's] fiction primarily through a Freudian lens, I do not want to reduce these works to Freudian paradigms or to suggest that the Freudian approach is the only way to make sense of these works [. . .] and I approach the Freudian material not as a way to psychoanalyze the author . . . but merely as one of the sources Faulkner [given " 'how omnivorously he read' "] mined, as he mined the Bible, Homer, Shakespeare and Dostoevsky" (p. 32).

xxvi Interpreting that "darkness": Morrison, pp. 149, 152.

xxvi "All of these images": Morrison, p. 147.

IMAGE OF BLACKS IN WESTERN ART

13 "White is the symbol": Albert Boime, *The Art of Exclusion: Representing Blacks in the Nineteenth Century* (Washington, DC: Smithsonian Institution Press, 1990), p. 3.

13 "In ancient Egypt": Boime, *Art of Exclusion,* p. 6.

17 Two texts, listed on the syllabus: Henri Baudet, *Paradise on Earth: Some Thoughts on European Images of Non-European Man,* trans. Elizabeth Wentholt (New Haven, CT: Yale University Press, 1965); and Roberto Fernández Retamar's essay "Caliban" in Roberto Fernández Retamar, *Caliban and Other Essays* (Minneapolis: University of Minnesota Press, 1989).

19 "According to unalterable": From Samuel Cartwright's paper in the *New Orleans Medical and Surgical Journal,* quoted in Sander L. Gilman, *On Blackness Without Blacks: Essays on the Image of the Black in Germany* (Boston: G. K. Hall, 1982) [emphasis added].

21 "Because language inhabits": Aldon Lynn Nielsen, *Reading Race: White American Poets and the Racial Discourse in the Twentieth Century* (Athens: University of Georgia Press, 1990).

THE SURROGATE SELF AS ENABLER

26   *metaphoric condensation*: See Sander L. Gilman, *Difference and Pathology: Stereotypes of Sexuality, Race, and Madness* (Ithaca, NY: Cornell University Press, 1985), pp. 132–37.

EDGAR ALLAN POE/HERMAN MELVILLE

33   "William Dunbar, seen": Bernard Bailyn, *Voyagers to the West: A Passage in the Peopling of America on the Eve of the Revolution* (New York: Knopf, 1985), pp. 488–489.

34   "Ever eager": Bailyn, *Voyagers to the West*, pp. 490–491.

34   "Dunbar, the young erudite": Bailyn, *Voyagers to the West*, p. 492.

35   "Constantly bewildered": Bailyn, *Voyagers to the West*, p. 491.

35   "a sense of authority": Bailyn, *Voyagers to the West*, p. 492.

39   "The dogma of the inferiority": Sander Gilman, *On Blackness Without Blacks: Essays on the Image of the Black in Germany* (Boston: G. K. Hall, 1982), pp. 10–11.

40   "Except for Negro slavery": Henry Adams, *The History of the United States of America*, vol. 1 (New York: Scribner's, 1909), p. 160.

40   *"seemed obliged"*: Constance Rourke, *American Humor: A Study of the National Character* (Garden City, NY: Doubleday, 1955), p. 36.

40   "The Yankee and the backwoodsman": Joyce Warren, *The American Narcissus: Individualism and Women in Nineteenth-Century American Fiction* (New Brunswick, NJ: Rutgers University Press, 1984), pp. 12–13.

40   "They appeared always": Rourke, *American Humor*, p. 144.

40   ideal picture of himself: See Warren, *American Narcissus*.

41   "After detailing the virtues": Warren, *American Narcissus*, p. 32.

41   "a great salesman": Warren, *American Narcissus*, p. 33.

41   he wrote that: Emerson paraphrased in Warren, *American Narcissus*, p. 33.

41   "Relationships with others": Warren, *American Narcissus*, p. 58.

41   "What he wanted": Warren, *American Narcissus*, p. 59.

42   "This inability": Warren, *American Narcissus*, p. 59.

42   "Hawthorne's best short": Irving Howe, *The American Newness: Culture and Politics in the Age of Emerson* (Cambridge, MA: Harvard University Press, 1986), p. 7.

42   *"Americans took the concept"*: Warren, *American Narcissus*, pp. 4–5 [italics in original].

43   "Transport yourself": Irving Howe, *The American Newness: Culture and Politics in the Age of Emerson* (Cambridge, MA: Harvard University Press, 1986), pp. 16–17.

43   "Here in the young": Howe, *American Newness*, p. 17.

44   "A corollary of manifest": Warren, *American Narcissus*, pp. 14–15.

44   "Governor Peter Chester": Bailyn, *Voyagers to the West*, pp. 482–483.

45   "To most Americans": Warren, *American Narcissus*, p. 15.

45   One of the most interesting: See Sander Gilman, *Difference and Pathology:*

Stereotypes of Sexuality, Race, and Madness (Ithaca, NY: Cornell University Press, 1985), pp. 132–137.

The following quotations in this lecture could not be definitively sourced in any of the works cited, or in any other lecture notes available in Toni Morrison's teaching archive. They are presented here as they appear in the surviving transcript.

45 "All of the terms of this description": Unverified; likely drawn from classroom notes or an oral reference.

46 "The great Romantics": (*Col. History.*) Parenthetical reference included in transcript; no exact source identified.

46 "Emerson exhorted his contemporaries": (*Col. History.*) Parenthetical reference included in transcript; no exact source identified.

ERNEST HEMINGWAY/WILLA CATHER

50 Joyce Warren's *American Narcissus:* See Joyce Warren, *The American Narcissus: Individualism and Women in Nineteenth-Century American Fiction* (New Brunswick, NJ: Rutgers University Press, 1984).

CARSON MCCULLERS

75 "These themes are never": Margaret C. McDowell, *Carson McCullers* (Boston: Twayne Publishers, 1980), p. 31.

77 See Frank Kermode's: Frank Kermode, *History and Value: The Clarendon Lectures and the Northcliffe Lectures* (Oxford: Clarendon Press, 1987).

79 See Margaret McDowell: McDowell, *Carson McCullers.*

HARRIET BEECHER STOWE

91 Alexander Saxton's article: See Alexander Saxton, *The Rise and Fall of the White Republic: Class Politics and Mass Culture in Nineteenth-Century America* (New York: Verso, 1990).

93 In a chapter called: See Terry Eagleton, *The Ideology of the Aesthetic* (Cambridge, MA: Blackwell, 1990), chap. 2, "The Law of the Heart: Shaftesbury, Hume, Burke," pp. 31–69.

93 "his [Shaftesbury's] unity": Eagleton, *Ideology of the Aesthetic,* p. 41.

93 "Legal, political and economic": Eagleton, *Ideology of the Aesthetic,* pp. 42–44.

MARK TWAIN

97 "reinsert a text": Dominick LaCapra, *History, Politics, and the Novel* (Ithaca, NY: Cornell University Press, 1987), p. 108.

98 "pertinent contexts": LaCapra, *History, Politics, and the Novel,* pp. 205–206.

100 "They have one great charm": Brander Matthews [Unsigned], "Review of *Huckleberry Finn,*" *Saturday Review,* Jan. 31, 1885; reprinted in *Huck Finn Among the Critics: A Centennial Selection* (Frederick, MD: University Publications of America, 1985), pp. 27–32 (31).

108 "I suggest that Mark Twain": V. S. Pritchett, *A Man of Letters* (New York: Random House, 1985), pp. 150–153.

WILLIAM FAULKNER

142 "The ideal of family life": *A History of Private Life: Riddles of Identity in Modern Times,* ed. Antoine Prost and Gérard Vincent, trans. Arthur Goldhammer (Cambridge, MA: Harvard University Press, 1991), pp. 541–543.

145 "basically a novel": Frederick R. Karl, *William Faulkner: American Writer* (New York: Ballantine Books, 1990), p. 446.

145 "The story is one": Karl, *Faulkner,* p. 447.

145 "about the murder": Karl, *Faulkner,* p. 504.

162 "A community of speakers": James A. Snead, *Figures of Division: William Faulkner's Major Novels* (New York: Methuen, 1986), p. 14.

SAUL BELLOW

172 "into the heart of darkness": Eusebio Rodrigues, *Quest for the Human: An Exploration of Saul Bellow's Fiction* (Lewisburg, PA: Bucknell University Press, 1981), p. 108.

173 "More basic is Bellow's": Rodrigues, *Quest for the Human,* pp. 110–111.

174 "The voice, the cry": Rodrigues, *Quest for the Human,* p. 113.

175 "Orgone therapy destroys": Rodrigues, *Quest for the Human,* pp. 123–124.

175 "Any inhibited aggressive rage": Rodrigues, *Quest for the Human,* p. 132.

175 "Teeth constitute": Rodrigues, *Quest for the Human,* p. 133.

175 "she has no pathological armor": Rodrigues, *Quest for the Human,* p. 124. (For following quotations and paraphrases of text from *Henderson,* see Bellow, pp. 72, 83–85, 185.)

176 "one may create": Rodrigues, *Quest for the Human,* p. 134.

176 "with sexual charm": Rodrigues, *Quest for the Human,* p. 139.

177 "What Henderson needs": Rodrigues, *Quest for the Human,* p. 142.

Index

Note: The terms "Africanistic" and "Africanist" are used interchangeably in the text. "Africanistic" is used in the index and encompasses both terms.

TONI MORRISON was the author of eleven novels and three essay collections. She received the National Book Critics Circle Award, the Pulitzer Prize, and in 1993 the Nobel Prize in Literature. She died in 2019.

CLAUDIA BRODSKY studied comparative literature at Harvard, Albert-Ludwigs University Freiburg, the Sorbonne, and Yale, where she taught German and comparative literature before joining the Comparative Literature Department at Princeton and serving as Program Director, International College of Philosophy, Paris. She is the author of *The Imposition of Form: Studies in Narrative Representation and Knowledge; Lines of Thought: Discourse, Architectonics, and the Origin of Modern Philosophy; In the Place of Language: Literature and the Architecture of the Referent; Words' Worth: What the Poet Does;* and *The Linguistic Condition: Kant's Critique of Judgment and the Poetics of Action,* as well as several dozen articles on philosophy and literature. She is editor of *Why Philosophy* and *Kant and Literary Studies* and co-editor with Toni Morrison of *Birth of a Nation'hood,* and with Eloy LaBrada of *Inventing Agency: Essays in the Literary and Philosophical Production of the Subject.*

A NOTE ON THE TYPE

This book was set in Adobe Garamond. Designed for the Adobe Corporation by Robert Slimbach, the fonts are based on types first cut by Claude Garamond (ca. 1480–1561). Garamond was a pupil of Geoffroy Tory and is believed to have followed the Venetian models, although he introduced a number of important differences, and it is to him that we owe the letter we now know as "old style." He gave to his letters a certain elegance and feeling of movement that won their creator an immediate reputation and the patronage of Francis I of France.

Typeset by Scribe,
Philadelphia, Pennsylvania

Designed by Cassandra J. Pappas